ANTHROPOLOGY
and the
Study of
HUMANITY

Scott M. Lacy, Ph.D.

THE
GREAT
COURSE

PUBLISHED BY:

THE GREAT COURSES
Corporate Headquarters
4840 Westfields Boulevard, Suite 500
Chantilly, Virginia 20151-2299
Phone: 1-800-832-2412
Fax: 703-378-3819
www.thegreatcourses.com

Scott M. Lacy, Ph.D.

Associate Professor of Sociology and Anthropology
Fairfield University

———————————————————————————————

S cott M. Lacy is an Associate Professor of Sociology and Anthropology at Fairfield University in Connecticut, where he teaches anthropology, environmental studies, and black studies courses. He is also the founder and executive director of African Sky, a nonprofit organization that serves hardworking farm families in rural Mali, West Africa. Dr. Lacy earned his Ph.D. in Anthropology at the University of California, Santa Barbara, where he started his teaching career in the Department of Black Studies as University of California President's Faculty

Fellow. Prior to arriving at his current post at Fairfield University, he taught in the Department of Anthropology at Emory University during his tenure as Marjorie Shostak Lecturer. Dr. Lacy's research interests include cross-cultural knowledge production, food systems, intellectual property rights associated with seed, and the anthropology of happiness.

Dr. Lacy has worked in Mali since 1994, when he first served in the Peace Corps. Since then, he has partnered with family farmers, teachers, community leaders, plant scientists, engineers, and a host of other knowledge specialists in Mali and throughout the world. A two-time Fulbright Scholar (in Mali from 2001–2002 and in Cameroon from 2016–2017), Dr. Lacy has presented his work as a consultant and/or keynote speaker for Engineers Without Borders, the Peace Corps, the Materials Research Society, ICRISAT Mali, the Institut d'Economie Rurale (Bamako, Mali), the Guangxi Maize Research Institute (Nanning, China), the D80 Conference, the Massachusetts Institute of Technology, and Columbia University. Dr. Lacy is working on a book manuscript that chronicles more than two decades of friendship and collaboration in southern Mali. His nonprofit and academic work has been featured in two major documentaries: *Sustaining Life* by Sprint Features (nominated for a 2009 Academy Award) and the 2017 release *Nyogonfe: Together*.

Dr. Lacy was awarded a Certificate of Congressional Recognition and Achievement from the US House of Representatives in 2011, the same year he was the inaugural awardee for Otterbein University's Global and Intercultural Engagement Award. He received a Martin Luther King, Jr. Humanitarian Award from Mothers On a Mission International and Strategic Solutions Group. Since his first years as a teacher, Dr. Lacy has received numerous teaching awards and grants from the University of California, Emory University, and Fairfield University. As an innovative instructor, he has mentored Institute for Developing Nations scholars (in Mali, Uganda, and Panama) through Emory University and The Carter Center. His applied teaching has resulted in a number of student projects, including documentary films, student research conferences, a West African drumming group, and a student-managed coffee cart that serves as an outpost for promoting sustainability.

Dr. Lacy is a coauthor of two popular textbooks, *Applying Anthropology* and *Applying Cultural Anthropology*, both published by McGraw-Hill. He has published a number of book chapters and articles that document cross-cultural knowledge production in agriculture, community development, engineering, and even nanotechnology. Dr. Lacy has appeared as a panelist on HuffPost Live and has been featured in newspapers and magazines, including *Sports Illustrated*. He is also known for his batik artwork, including one piece that toured the country from 2006 to 2009 as part of a traveling Smithsonian Folklife Festival exhibit celebrating the US National Park Service. ∎

Table of Contents

Unit 2: Sole Survivors

Unit 3: Human Diversity

Unit 4: Applying Anthropology

SUPPLEMENTAL MATERIAL

Anthropology and the Study of Humanity

Anthropology is an interdisciplinary field that is uniquely positioned to answer some of humanity's biggest questions: Who are we? Where do we come from? And how could it be that, despite our seemingly limitless physical and cultural diversity, we are indeed a single human race? Anthropologists hold no monopoly on truth or explanations, but they do employ a wide range of methods to explore the remarkable breadth of the human condition.

This course is an introduction to academic anthropology and its 4 subfields: biological anthropology, archaeology, linguistics, and sociocultural anthropology. Over the course of 24 lectures, we will learn how anthropology and its subfields further our understanding of our world and ourselves. Specifically, we'll see how anthropologists deploy multidisciplinary methods to trace the origins of our species as well as the development of religion, agriculture, money, language, and many other pillars of the modern human experience.

Our anthropological journey is organized into 4 units. First, we begin with biological anthropology to address the question: Who are we, and where do we come from? Specifically, unit 1 focuses on biological anthropology, which studies the origins of humanity, primatology, the spread of humankind, and a re-articulation of the concept of race.

In unit 2, we move to the question of our status as the sole remaining survivors of a long line of upright walking apes. In particular, we bring in archaeology and linguistics to work out how *Homo sapiens* outlived all the other branches of our extended family tree. This exploration reveals how tools, agriculture, cities, money, and language all contributed to the survival of our species.

In unit 3, we turn to cultural anthropology to explore why people and cultures are so diverse despite our singularity as a species. We'll review the history and methods of cultural anthropology and see differences in the way people throughout the world practice and understand core pieces of humanity, including family, marriage, gender, sexuality, religion, and artistic expression.

Finally, in unit 4, we'll apply all 4 subfields of anthropology to see how this interdisciplinary approach helps us understand and work out human problems. We'll see anthropologists in action as they examine conflict, forensics, health, economic development, ecology, and even the nature and pursuit of happiness.

In sum, we will discover that anthropology digs deep into the geographic, temporal, and biological diversity of humankind to help us understand our remarkable diversity as a species. And ironically, the deeper we dig, the more we reveal the oneness of the human race.

Why Anthropology Matters

I t's helpful to start any study of anthropology with a definition of what anthropology is. Put simply, anthropology is the study of humankind over time and space. American Anthropology is categorized into 4 subfields: biological anthropology, archaeology, linguistics, and cultural anthropology. We use each of these subfields to explore the survival and diversity of humankind across time and geography. This opening lecture will launch our anthropological journey by describing what anthropology is and how it produces knowledge that matters.

Subfields

The first subfield, biological anthropology, includes everything from primatology and paleontology to evolution, biology, genetics, health, and forensic science. All of those themes will be covered in the early lectures of the course, as we answer the big questions: Who are we, and where do we come from?

The next subfield, archaeology, uncovers and interprets artifacts to reveal the histories of people who are no longer here to share their stories. Like crime scene detectives, we can look at what earlier humans left behind to work out how they lived and died.

The third subfield, linguistic anthropology, is much more than studying languages. Linguists dissect the structure of language; preserve and investigate dead languages; tell language histories; and provide a record of human migrations and cultural interaction.

Finally, cultural anthropology is an interdisciplinary subfield that explores kinship, economics, gender, development, religion, art, and just about anything else we humans do. Through cultural anthropology, we'll explore how, despite cultural and linguistic differences, we are a single human race.

While anthropologists typically specialize in 1 or more of these subfields, the lines between them are blurry. In fact, most anthropologists draw on several or all 4 subfields to investigate our world.

Applied Anthropology and Building Bridges

One technique that focuses on real-world uses for anthropology is applied anthropology. Applied anthropologists tend to differ from conventional academic researchers. In addition to traditional academic tasks, applied anthropologists may write annual reports for charities or research institutes, they may help draft legislation, or they might bring various stakeholders together to improve patient outcomes at a regional clinic.

There are countless examples of anthropologists who consider themselves applied anthropologists, and there's an even larger number with interdisciplinary training and scholarship. Some of the biggest areas of applied and/or interdisciplinary anthropology include medical anthropology, legal anthropology, education, and international development.

Anthropologists can act as bridge builders between cultures. It's in that capacity that they're able to produce cross-cultural knowledge, that is, knowledge that draws on the experience and understanding of diverse groups who often have no common cultural ground.

Such knowledge is important because it counteracts the problem of cultural bias and blind spots in order to create benefits for a wider swath of humanity. And perhaps even more starkly, such an approach works to mitigate the power inequalities imbued in top-down development programs.

A Field Experiment

By looking at a field experiment that took place in the village of Dissan in Mali, we can see anthropology at work as a cross-cultural knowledge producer. Sorghum is a major crop in Dissan. The experiment involved 23

new varieties of sorghum collected from ICRISAT, the International Crops Research Institute for the Semi-Arid Tropics. Near Bamako, Mali, they have a research station with a well-respected sorghum-breeding program.

The participant observer had a packet of seed for all 23 varieties, plus a local variety of their choosing. Together, the participant observer apprenticed with each participating family, and used a handheld hoe to plant individual parcels of each test variety. They did 5-square-meter plots and planted 8 rows of sorghum in each plot.

They marked each parcel to identify the 24 varieties and planted all 24 packets right in the middle of the participant families' fields. The center of fields tends to be the richest, more productive parts of fields in Dissan.

The study was published in the journal *Agriculture and Human Values*, but here are some of the big takeaways:

- Unlike the official trials plots, farmers tend to test novel sorghum varieties on the perimeters of their family fields. That's because they eat what they grow, so when they test seed, they don't have the luxury of giving up their most productive spots: the centers of their family sorghum fields.

- One farmer explained that he looks for new varieties that perform despite less than perfect conditions. That's because if they work well in bad spots, they'll emerge as champions elsewhere in the field.

- Farmers insisted on intercropping the test varieties in their secondary plots. They explained that they needed to give the seed a chance. Beans and other legumes fix nitrogen in the soil, much to the delight of sorghum.

- The farmers not only loved the experiment, after the test plots, they adopted the exact opposite sorghum varieties from their stated preferences. Before planting, the households said they preferred heavy seed, but after, they adopted 5 of the 8 lightest varieties available and only 2 of the 8 heaviest varieties.

- The farmers also said they preferred varieties that

Sorghum

matured quickly in 3 months or less. However, they adopted only 1 of the 3 fastest varieties available and 4 of the 5 slowest. This observation demonstrates the importance of engaged, long-term field research. Like everyone else, these farmers don't always say what they do or do what they say.

Information like this is indispensible for the development of national and international plant-breeding programs. Scientists can't just ask family farmers like those in Dissan to make a list of desired seed traits. That's a good start, but such a list will be incomplete.

Cross-cultural projects in particular require participant observation and other anthropological approaches. Anthropology is a tool for social transformation. It's a means to creating stronger communities and a happier, healthier world.

Suggested Reading

Bernard, *Research Methods in Anthropology*.

Lacy, "Nanotechnology and Food Security."

Podolefsky, Brown, and Lacy, *Applying Anthropology*.

Questions to Consider

1. What are the 4 subfields of anthropology, and what does each subfield investigate?

2. Why is bridge building an effective metaphor for the work and relevance of anthropology?

Science, Darwin, and Anthropology

As humans, it's in our nature to ask big questions. And as a meaning-seeking species, perhaps the biggest question we can ask is: Who are we, and where do we come from? In this lecture, we'll consider how people have answered this question over the past 3,000 years or so. First, we'll look at prescientific and nonscientific ideas. Then, we'll see how the emergence of science, including anthropology, completely changed the way we understand ourselves and our origins.

Prescientific Answers

Long before the emergence of science, humanity had woven a rich tapestry of colorful origin stories and folktales to give meaning and order to the world.

An example comes from the Channel Islands just off the coast of Santa Barbara. There, the ancestors of the Chumash people gave an answer to the question, "Who are we, and where do we come from?"

Before the age of microscopes and Bunsen burners, the ancestors gave an answer with certainty, but they really didn't concern themselves with empirical proof. In this case, the answer was that a female deity named Hutash planted seeds on Santa Cruz Island, and those seeds grew into the first people.

Spectacularly, Hutash created a rainbow bridge for people to cross over the Pacific to the mainland of California. And those who made it over are the ancestors of contemporary Chumash people. But those who fell into the ocean became dolphins.

Positivism and a History of Science

The philosopher Auguste Comte examined how people have answered the big human questions over time. Ultimately, he spelled out an evolutionary schema to explain how humanity developed into the scientific knowledge producers we are today.

Comte's schema goes under the name of positivism, which identifies 3 main stages in the human quest for truth: the theological phase, the metaphysical phase, and the positive phase.

In the theological phase of human development, humans associated the unknown exclusively with unpredictable supernatural forces like the gods of ancient Greece. Blaming Zeus or someone else in the pantheon mollified humans because they had an explanation for what's going on, and the human mind craves explanations.

Eventually, however, humankind transitioned into another phase on the road to scientific knowledge: the metaphysical phase. In this phase, thinkers like Aristotle used reason and observation to sharpen their understanding of the world. Aristotle theorized that the universe consisted of 3 types of substances: earthly matter that can be seen and felt; celestial matter that can be seen but not felt; and spirit matter that can't be seen or felt.

This explanation of the universe traveled widely, from Thomas Aquinas in the Christian tradition, to Averroes and Maimonides of the Muslim and Jewish traditions, respectively. All of these influential thinkers incorporated Aristotle's explanation of the cosmos. Simply put, they did this because Aristotle's explanation placed the earth at the center of the cosmos, surrounded by the heavens. It required a prime mover or deity.

Aristotle's ideas about the universe held strong well into the Middle Ages, largely because they aligned so well with existing religious explanations of the universe. But eventually, people like Galileo picked up instruments like telescopes and determined that the earth couldn't possibly be at the center of the universe.

A critical invention that inspired people like Galileo to test and correct our knowledge of the universe came from mid-1500s Europe. That's when and where Johannes Gutenberg built a printing press that, unlike the wood and ceramic print blocks that preceded it, made viable the mass production of books.

Amazingly, without cars, trains, or factories, the Gutenberg press spread across Europe in half a century. A faster and cheaper way of making books meant that humans had progressively more books, and therefore more access to information.

Charles Darwin

The anthropological elder Charles Darwin noticed that humans are related to every living organism. He wasn't the first person to come up with that idea, though. His grandfather, Erasmus Darwin, wrote *Zoonomia* some 60 years before Charles Darwin's *On the Origin of Species*. And the ideas in that text will sound quite familiar to readers of *Origin of Species*, namely, that all living organisms share a common ancestor.

Just before the elder Darwin started writing, a naturalist

Charles Darwin

named Carl Linnaeus began publishing *Systema Naturae* in 1735. In this multivolume classic, Linnaeus classified any living thing he could set his eyes on. In essence, he gave us our very first comprehensive family tree of all living organisms.

One question that challenged Erasmus Darwin and Linnaeus alike was the question of how species emerge. They could see and classify the planet's biological diversity, but they weren't clear on the actual mechanisms of evolution.

In the testable and correctable tradition of science, Charles Darwin picked up the mantel and continued the efforts of his grandfather. Darwin explained that the mechanism of evolution is natural selection. Specifically, organisms change gradually over time. As a result sometimes new species emerge, and sometimes they die out.

He broke this process down into 4 pieces:

1. Within a single species, there is variation in traits. Imagine, for example, starfish in the Caribbean. Some are red, but some are pinkish and barely visible because they blend so well into the ocean floor.
2. Not all of these starfish will be equally successful at reproducing. Darwin called this differential reproduction. Sea creatures like manta rays and a few types of sharks love eating up starfish. And because they can easily spot the red ones, it's the red ones that tend to get eaten unlike their camouflaged counterpart. As a result, fewer red starfish survive to reproduce.
3. Additionally, there is heredity. The pink starfish transmit their pink color to their offspring, as do the red ones provided that some diver or shark does not snatch them up.
4. In our ocean water example, the pink starfish color is an advantageous trait because it reduces the likelihood of being discovered by a predator. As time rolls on, the pink starfish become the most common

type of these starfish, until eventually it is the sole survivor.

Testing and Correcting

Unlike the Chumash origin story, Darwin's answers were produced through science. That means his answers were contingent truths that scientists were supposed to test and correct. And that's exactly what people did.

One of the earliest revisions of Darwin's ideas came from Gregor Mendel, a monk living in what is now the Czech Republic. Darwin theorized that heredity operates through blending: An organism is a blend of its 2 parents.

Mendel knew about cross-breeding plants to produce desirable traits like high yields. Mendel planted huge numbers of pea plants at his monastery to test his ideas about how traits pass from parent to offspring.

Mendel observed 7 key traits of his plants. He watched how traits like pod color were expressed in 1 of only 2 ways: yellow or green. Mendel noticed that only 1 of 4 plants tended to have yellow pods.

He noted the same ratio for other traits like seed shape and plant height. What he discovered were dominant and recessive genes. A yellow pod is rare because it only emerges when both parents contribute a recessive gene for pod color; any other combination produces green.

Mendel wasn't the only person testing, correcting, and improving our understanding of evolution. Hugo de Vries helped us begin to imagine and test ideas about mutations, Francis Crick and James Watson revealed to us the structure of DNA, and now we've mapped out the entire human genome.

Social Darwinism

It didn't take long for people to metaphorically apply the idea of evolution outside the biological world. Influenced by Darwin's ideas, scholars like Herbert Spencer and William H. McGee ushered in social Darwinism, which asserted that social systems and cultures travel the same trajectory as evolving plants and animals do: They go from simple to complex.

In the late 19th century, social Darwinism ruled the day because it was considered a "scientific" way to explain and justify some serious inconsistencies and inequalities on the planet. Simply enough, people were poor because they were less evolved.

The arrival of social-Darwinist thinking emerged with the arrival of the earliest anthropologists. While other biologists sorted out the rest of the animal kingdom, this new field called anthropology tried to make sense of human diversity, biological and cultural.

Harvard's own Frederick Ward Putnam revealed the new discipline to the American public at the Chicago World's Fair in 1893, which included an anthropology exhibit. The fair was a celebration of technology in the new scientific age.

Among other sights, there was a pair of marble statues to represent the "ideal" man and woman. The sculptures were created based on measurements taken from Harvard and Radcliffe students. Putnam and others were imposing the biological model of evolution upon culture and cultural achievements.

Today, we consider this idea to be the very definition of ethnocentrism and pseudoscience, but back then, people were essentially arguing that some people are further

along on the evolutionary path, biologically and culturally.

Such thinking was embraced by those who could then justify disastrous inequalities like colonization and manifest destiny as moral burdens. Rather than understanding colonization and the Atlantic slave trade as evil-rooted violence, whites of European extraction believed they had a moral duty to extend their colonial reach, no matter the human cost.

More Testing and Correcting

Biological determinism and social-Darwinist thinking were so pervasive at the dawn of the 20th century that their influence even reached into the Supreme Court of the United States.

In 1896, just as anthropology was emerging as an academic discipline, the Supreme Court justices consulted the science of the day and upheld racial segregation as constitutional in the *Plessy v. Ferguson* case.

In line with the day's anthropological theories, Justice Henry Brown wrote the majority decision and said that so long as one race was inferior to the other, the Constitution is powerless to put them on the same plane.

Justice John Marshall Harlan's dissent saw the upholding of segregation as planting seeds of racial hate, but he was clearly in the minority. So, just like their anthropology contemporaries, most of the Supreme Court justices used science and prevailing ideas about evolution to defend racial inequalities as "natural" and segregation as inevitable.

There's a silver lining that has been at work throughout this lecture: the testable and correctable nature of science. We're always learning more.

Suggested Reading

Bolotin and Laing, *The World's Columbian Exposition*.

Darwin, *The Origin of Species*.

Newkirk, *Spectacle*.

Stocking, *Victorian Anthropology*.

Questions to Consider

1. Beyond survival of the fittest, what is natural selection and how does it work?

2. What is social Darwinism and why did it become so influential on the edge of the 20th century?

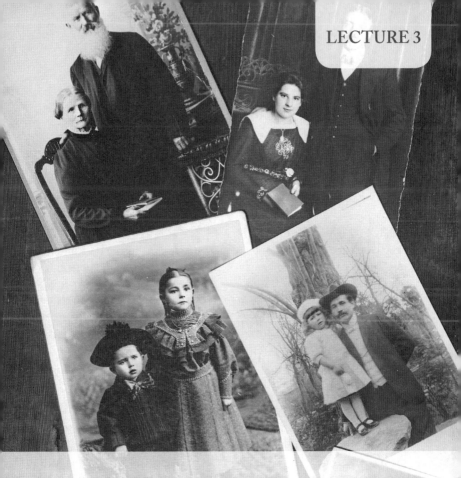

Our Primate Family Tree

T his lecture travels back in time over 63 million years to introduce an ancestor shared by every living primate on Earth today. In this course, we've looked at how, over the past few thousand years, people have answered the question: Who are we, and where do we come from? This lecture shows what the primate order has to say about that big question. It starts by considering how and why anthropologists integrate primatology into our study of humankind, and then takes a closer look at our primate family tree.

We Are Primates

Humans have a long and amazing line of primate ancestors. The more we interact with and study our primate cousins, the more we see the depths of our shared genetic heritage.

A remarkable study from the Yerkes National Primate Research Center at Emory University shows the human-like depths of our primate cousins. The researchers did a simple game with capuchin monkeys. Two monkeys side by side in separate cages took turns trading marbles for food treats. They were trained to give a marble to the research assistant in order to receive a food treat, starting with grapes.

As the experiment went on, one of the monkeys began receiving inferior cucumber bites instead of grapes, while the other began receiving more grapes. The one receiving cucumber bites began to react angrily, showing a human like reaction: discontent at unfair treatment.

From our behavioral similarities down to our shared genetic heritage, nonhuman primates can teach us so much about being human. In some cases, these differences begin to disappear the more we probe them. That's exciting because we're getting more and more precise about what it means to be human.

Susan Savage-Rumbaugh

Primatologists collect data and test theories to help us understand our humanity, including our primate roots. Generally, primatologists tend to specialize in one or more areas, from primate genetics and anatomy, to cognition, behavior, and social organization.

To get a better idea of what primatologists think about, this lecture will visit 2 exceptional primatologists to see them in action. First up is Susan Savage-Rumbaugh, an exceptional primatologist known for cognitive and behavioral research.

Her star collaborator in this research is a bonobo ape named Kanzi. As a bonobo, Kanzi shares almost 99% of our genome, and together, Susan Savage-Rumbaugh and Kanzi definitely teach us that our human-bonobo differences could be more cultural than they are biological.

Kanzi lives at a primate research center in Iowa, and he's helped us test language as one of the boundaries between humans and the other apes. Susan Savage-Rumbaugh and Kanzi speak through lexigrams or symbols representing words, but Kanzi clearly understands Savage-Rumbaugh's spoken English.

Videos exist of Kanzi and Savage-Rumbaugh making a campfire. As Kanzi methodically completes one task at a time, Savage-Rumbaugh talks to him with helpful banter. She reminds him that there's a lighter in her pocket, after which Kanzi digs in and grabs it.

Kanzi not only builds, lights, and tends a true campfire: He also makes a s'more with a toasted marshmallow and puts the fire out with a bucket of water. He demonstrated a curious ability to remember and manage complex tasks.

Capuchin monkey

Laurie Santos

This lecture's second primatologist is Laurie Santos at Yale. After the economic collapse of 2008, Santos wondered if other primates share human inclinations toward risky economic behavior. She found that they definitely do.

Santos and her students taught primates how to use money to buy snacks. Then, in a series of experiments, she tested their financial strategies by setting up a monkey market.

First, the researchers taught capuchin monkeys to use money. They gave the monkeys a wallet with a dozen aluminum coins, which they used to trade for food. At the monkey market, the capuchins eventually got to make a choice between 1 of 2 snacks.

Then Santos kicked it up a notch. Prices at the monkey market changed, and some choices were cheaper than others. So, are capuchin monkeys bargain hunters like us? Santos and her research tell us yes.

Additionally, Santos never saw a monkey save coins for the future.

They love shopping and eating, and they seem as human as us when it comes to blowing the budget.

Shared DNA

Now that we've seen primatologists in action, let's get back to the primate family tree through the lens of genetics and biology. When we explore our origins, genetics can dramatically change the way we understand our place in the world. Remarkably, we share a surprising number of genes with all living things.

Let's take a tour of the primate family to see how and where we stack up to our remarkable cousins. In essence, we need to figure out how a common ancestor could eventually evolve into such a wide variety of primates, including humans.

There are 3 major types of primates: prosimians, monkeys, and apes. Technically, humans fit into the ape category. Nonetheless, we all share a common ancestor. We've all been on the same evolutionary freeway, and the only reason why chimpanzees are different from orangutans and humans is that we each took different exits to continue our evolutionary journey.

One important note: This is not to say that humans were once chimpanzees. We share a common relative with modern chimpanzees.

Prosimians and the MRCA

Now, it's time to meet the common ancestor shared by primates. Her name is MRCA, an acronym for most recent common ancestor. This MRCA kind of looked like a squirrel with a long tail.

In the world inhabited by the MRCA more than 60 million years ago, there were none of the current primates because they hadn't evolved just yet. Instead, proto-primates were living an arboreal lifestyle in the trees.

Ultimately, some proto-primates splintered off to become the prosimian branch of our family tree. Just over 60 million years ago the first prosiminans—the lemurs and lorises—diverged from the rest of the primates, and then the tarsiers broke off a few million years later.

Lemurs, lorises, and tarsiers are all prosimians, but the tarsiers are closer cousins to humans because they stayed on the evolutionary freeway for those extra few million years. Prosimians are small, often nocturnal primates with large eyes. Some of them leap through the trees while others are skilled climbers.

Lemurs, like all prosimians, used to be found in many places, but now the only lemur populations are in Madagascar. The smallest lemurs, like the dwarf lemur, would easily fit in the palm of a human hand. But larger lemurs, like sifakas, can weigh up to about 15 pounds.

Outside of Madagascar, the other prosimians—lorises and tarsiers— are found in Africa, India, and Southeast Asia. They too are mainly nocturnal tree-dwellers who are usually strong climber or jumpers.

New World and Old World Monkeys

As the prosimians continued to evolve on their own, the rest of the primates carried on down the evolutionary freeway until the next

Lemur

group broke off on its own. First the New World monkeys broke off some 40 million years ago, and then the Old World monkeys followed suit around 15 million years later.

Let's take a look at the Platyrrhini, another term for the New World monkeys. New World monkeys can be found in Central and South America. They're tree-dwellers and

they like to eat leaves, fruit, and occasionally insects.

On the small end of the Platyrrhini spectrum are the marmoset and tamarins. They can't change their facial expressions, they don't have opposable thumbs, and they frequently produce twins. Once those twins are born, males tend to carry infants on their back when the children aren't nursing.

The bigger side of the New World Monkey classification is the Cebidae family. These monkeys are also limited to Central and South America, but they are much larger than the marmosets. The howler monkey, for example, can grow to over 20 pounds.

With the New World monkeys and the prosimians departed, the rest of the early primates moved on together, further down the primate evolution freeway. They were becoming more and more human all along the way.

Take the Old World monkeys. Humans have much more in common with Old World monkeys than we do with prosimians and new world monkeys. Take teeth, for example. Humans have 8 teeth on each side of each jaw.

Old World monkeys also have 8 teeth per side. This is different from the New World monkeys, who have 9. Humans also have the same types of teeth as the Old World monkeys: 2 incisors first, then a canine tooth, then 2 premolars, and then 3 molars. The New World monkeys have an extra premolar that Old World monkeys and humans got rid of.

Old World monkeys can be found in Africa, the Middle East, and parts of Asia. Baboons and macaques are examples of Old World monkeys. Driving home the depths of our shared genetic path through evolution, the rhesus macaque is the most frequently used primate in human medical research.

Apes

With the prosimians, Old World monkeys, and New World monkeys branched off, all that is left is the apes. Things picked up quickly for the earliest apes. Around 17–18 million years ago, the gibbons took off on their own path. The orangutan and gorilla did the same a few million years after that.

Around 7 million years ago, humans left the common evolutionary path. That left the bonobo and chimpanzee to split up on their own. This explains why we share some 99% of our genome with the bonobo and chimpanzee, but only 80% or so with the lemur. Humans, chimps, and bonobos were together the longest on the primate evolution freeway.

Suggested Reading

De Waal, *The Bonobo and the Atheist.*

Goodall, *In the Shadow of Man.*

Sterling, Bynum, and Blair, *Primate Ecology and Conservation.*

Questions to Consider

1. How does learning about the primate order help us understand what it means to be human?

2. What are some fascinating similarities and stark differences between us humans and the rest of the primate family?

3. What are the origins of the primate order, and where exactly do humans fit among the other primates?

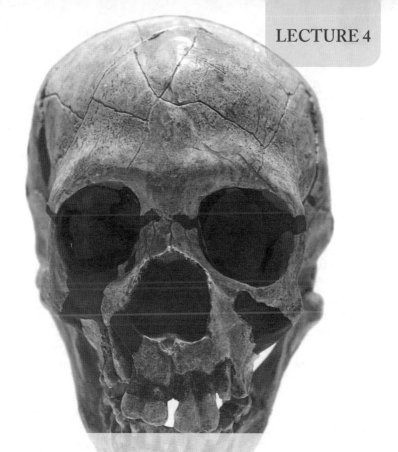

Paleoanthropology and the Hominin Family

T his lecture introduces more knowledge about the primate
family tree. Already, we've gained insight into human origins by
looking at the field of primatology. In this lecture, we'll turn to
paleoanthropology to trace our earliest human ancestors through to modern
Homo sapiens. Like primatology, paleoanthropology will give us some
great perspective as we explore answers to our foundational anthropology
question: Who are we, and where do we come from?

Recent Arrivals

Humans are relatively recent arrivals. The Earth is 4.5 billion years old. Humans began to diverge from our closest primate cousins around 7 million years ago.

From a paleoanthropologic point of view, the moment our ancestors started walking on 2 feet demarcates our human origins as primates. Paleoanthropologists are the human origins specialists in the anthropology family. They search for paleoecological evidence, namely fossil evidence, to reveal details about the lives and biology of the earliest humans.

Paleoanthropologists teach us that the earliest apes who started walking upright lived some 7 million years ago. Slowly, over time, hominins (upright walking apes who are direct human ancestors) evolved into modern humans.

Sahelanthropus tchadensis

In Chad in central Africa, the researcher Michel Brunet and his team made a game-changing paleoanthropological discovery. They unearthed a famous fossil that is certainly one of the earliest hominins on the human family tree.

In 2001, Brunet's team discovered the remains of a primate skull that dates back some 6–7 million years. The skull ended up being identified as *Sahelanthropus tchadensis*.

Sahelanthropus tchadensis is remarkable because:

● It dates back to the same timeframe humans separated from the chimpanzees and bonobos.
● This early primate was likely a facultative bipedal. In other words, it walked on 2 feet.
● It's our oldest known primate ancestor whose fossil remains indicate that it was bipedal. And that is where we started our human story: with these earliest upright-walking apes.

An important question: How can someone look at a skull and determine if a primate ancestor walked on 2 feet?

● When all we have is just a skull, a major indicator for bidpedalism can be seen in the foramen magnum—the

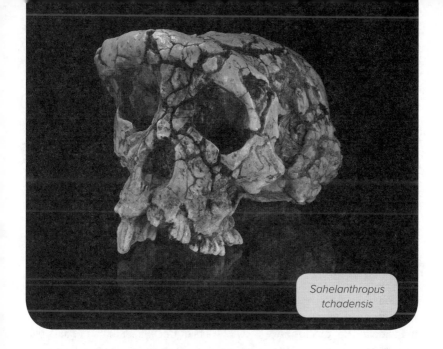

place where the skull meets the spine. In a gorilla or chimpanzee skull, the foramen magnum is toward the rear of the skull, not the center, as it is with humans.

- Bipeds have a more centrally located foramen magnum than nonhuman primate relatives. So does *Sahelanthropus*.

Ultimately, Brunet and his colleagues argue that this fossil is one of our earliest bipedal ancestors, close to the time we split from chimpanzees and bonobos. Some think *Sahelanthropus* was more of a peripheral human ancestor, and others challenge both of these arguments because of a dearth of any other evidence.

Ardipithecus

East of Chad toward Ethiopia, other paleoanthropologists, Timothy White and Berhane Asfaw, discovered one of the earliest known fossils of our human ancestors. Beginning in the early 1990s, Asfaw and White's team began uncovering some extremely fragile fossil remains. They were so delicate that it took 15 years to preserve and analyze what they found. They also had to do CT scans to make it easier to piece together the fragmented remains.

Their results were groundbreaking. Their major find was the skeletal remains of a female who lived 4.4 million years ago. She was bipedal, but she could get around in the trees as well. Scientists dubbed this new discovery *Ardipithecus ramidus*.

In the late 1990s and into the 2000s, Yohannes Haile-Selassie discovered more fossil evidence of *Ardipithecus* in Ethiopia. The remains he unearthed were confirmed as part of the *Ardipithecus* classification, but were an older type that lived over 5.5 million years ago. They named this early human ancestor *Ardipithecus kadabba* because *kadabba* means "oldest ancestor" in the local Afar language.

Raymond Dart and *Australopithecus africanus*

From time to time, humans have found fossils that beg further inquiry. Take Raymond Dart, for example. Dart was a professor of anatomy living in South Africa in the early 20th century.

One day Dart came across a captivating fossil. It was a skull with jawbone. It was relatively complete, and Dart knew something was odd about his find. It clearly wasn't a modern human, but it certainly didn't resemble any other modern ape. Its skull, for example, was smaller than a human skull, but larger than a chimpanzee's.

The skull was named the Taung child: "Taung" because of the town in South Africa where it was found by quarry workers in 1924, and "child" because it turns out that this specimen died as a child. In fact, we're pretty sure that the Taung child died as the result of an eagle attack.

Dart proposed we classify this skull as *Australopithecus africanus* (meaning "southern ape from Africa"). Distinct from humans and other primates, this represents another major era on our evolutionary timeline and our evolutionary family tree.

In the case of the Taung child discovery, and Dart's theory that it represents a major moment in our evolutionary path, anthropologists challenged and tested these ideas rigorously.

At first, many were skeptical of the idea that *Australopithecus* was a direct human ancestor, but over the decades, more and more fossils emerged to support the theory that at least some australopithecines were indeed a direct ancestor of *Homo sapiens*.

Ultimately we've learned that these australopithecines lived some 4 million years ago in Africa, largely eastern Africa.

There were many types. *Australopithecus afarensis*, for example, is definitely a direct human ancestor. Perhaps the most famous of all the australopithecines is Lucy, a female *Australopithecus afarensis*. Her discovery in 1974 was celebrated widely because it is rare to find such an old yet fairly complete and well-preserved skeleton.

Homo habilis

Just as Raymond Dart analyzed the Taung child fossil and concluded it didn't fit any existing classification, the same thing happened to the famous paleontologists Mary and Louis Leakey.

In the early 1960s, the Leakeys found the remains of an early human that caught their attention. It wasn't a modern human, but it wasn't an *Australopithecus* either. It was somewhere in between. Its brain and body was a little larger, and it lived more recently than our *Australopithecus* ancestors.

The Leakeys created a new intermediary classification that clarifies our path from *Sahelanthropus* to *Homo sapiens*. Additional discoveries throughout East Africa affirmed the status of this newly revealed ancestor: *Homo habilis*, or "handy human."

Homo habilis lived in Africa about 2.5 million years ago. Their brain size had grown. Researchers have found *Homo habilis* remains with very crude stone tools, something they had yet to find with earlier ancestors like *Ardipithecus*.

Homo erectus

The next ancestor on the timeline is *Homo erectus*. The first known *Homo erectus* discovery was found in 1891 by a Dutch surgeon, Eugène Dubois, who clearly saw it was not human. Like Dart and the Leakeys,

Dubois created a new classification for his ape-like skull discovery. He called it *Pithecanthropus erectus* ("ape who stands erect"). Later fossils filled in the gap of our knowledge, and eventually paleoanthropologists modified the name of this ancestor to *Homo erectus*.

The first *Homo erectus* populations appeared just under 2 million years ago. Their cranial capacity could exceed 1000 cubic centimeters, clearly a major leap beyond the 750 cubic centimeters of *Homo habilis*. These ancestors had quite an amazing toolkit compared with everyone who came before them. And *Homo erectus* can be found outside of Africa.

Some scientists separate the *Homo erectus* populations into three distinct groups based on their geographic distribution: *Homo ergaster* (Africa); *Homo erectus* (Asia); and *Homo heidelbergensis* (Europe).

Archaic Homo sapiens

Homo erectus appeared 1.9 million years ago and went extinct as recently as 150,000 years ago.

Somewhere out of that *Homo erectus* population emerged archaic *Homo sapiens*.

The archaic form of *Homo sapiens* first came into the fossil record when the Leakeys found some remains dated over 100,000 years ago. That was 1967. Contemporary teams have revisited the fossils and the site; they dated these early *Homo sapiens* to around 190,000 years ago. The most celebrated fossils are called the Omo skulls, and they're our oldest known definitively *Homo sapiens* fossils.

As of yet, we've only found early *Homo sapiens* fossils in eastern Africa, leading us to believe that modern humans are likely rooted to a population of *Homo sapiens* who lived in Africa before spreading out to the other continents.

Testing and Correcting: The Hobbit

Anthropologists are never satisfied with stagnant theories. They test and retest their theories and ideas. One recent "test-and-correct" challenge they've dealt with relates to the "hobbit," a small human that lived in Indonesia within the past 20,000 years or so.

After the bones of this small, recent human were discovered in 2003, the popular press labeled it a hobbit. The scientific name was *H. floresiensis* because their remains were found on the island of Flores.

Specifically, this was a population of 1-meter-tall hominins who not only had a complex tool kit, but lived long after we thought every hominin species but *Homo sapiens* had gone extinct. And they had relatively small brains for being such sharp toolmakers.

The hobbits mess up the clean storyline of better tools through bigger brains as the road to survival as well as the old idea about humans being the sole remaining hominins for the past 40,000 years.

For now, most folks tend to keep our hominin-evolution storylines in tact by subscribing to 1 of 2 theories:

1.   Some people argue that the small humans are smaller simply because of a genetic condition that emerged in the region and remained isolated.

2. Another theory states that on a small island with limited resources, larger animals like humans would likely evolve to become smaller to better compete for limited resources.

Regardless, the fossil record is clear and it's deep. Walking upright appears to have been a game changer for us, and in many ways, we can consider bipedalism as the foundation of our humanity, biological and otherwise.

Suggested Reading

Dawkins and Yan, *The Ancestor's Tale*.

Tattersall, *Masters of the Planet*.

Questions to Consider

1. When did the first upright walking apes migrate beyond Africa?

2. How were our pre-*Homo sapiens* ancestors different from modern humans?

3. What are some examples of groundbreaking fossil discoveries that help us construct our early history as upright walking apes?

Tracing the Spread of Humankind

The previous lecture retraced our origins to the first bipedal apes some 7 million years ago. Remarkably, we *Homo sapiens* are the sole survivors of what used to be a vastly diverse hominin family tree. This lecture adds to our human story by bringing in some geography to retrace the spread of humankind. Specifically, we'll see how humans migrated into just about every corner of the world, including the Americas. Starting in East Africa, we'll watch *Homo sapiens* spread into the Middle East, Asia, Europe, and eventually the Americas.

Naia

In 2007, a software engineer and his avid scuba diver friends accidently discovered one of the oldest human skeletons ever found in the Americas.

They named her Naia, after the Naiads, who were mythical Greek water nymphs. Naia may have been alone the past 12,000 years, but she was one of the very first Americans.

Naia's presence on the Yucatan Peninsula tells us that humans have been in the Americas for at least 12,000 to 13,000 years. Her remains rank among the oldest, most complete human skeletons ever discovered in the Americas.

Homo erectus

After over a century of revolutionary fossil discoveries, we now have a clear idea of when the first hominins migrated out of Africa. Appearing nearly 2 million ago, *Homo erectus* fossils line the trail of their collective migrations into the Middle East, Europe, and Asia. They showed up in Java about 1.8 million years ago, and in Europe and Asia not long after that.

The Zhoukoudian site near Beijing, for example, has produced fossilized remains from some 40 different *Homo erectus* individuals. Those fossils and others show us that by 800k years ago, Homo erectus was living as far as Southeast Asia, the Middle East, and southern Europe.

Homo erectus, however, has been extinct for 400,000 years, and unlike *Homo sapiens*, they never made it to northern Asia, northern Europe, or the Americas.

Three Theories

After *Homo erectus* went extinct, it was up to *Homo sapiens* to settle the rest of the globe. But why did *Homo erectus* go extinct after spreading across Africa and into southern Asia and Europe? How did *Homo sapiens* come to populate the world? Three major theories seek to answer these questions:

1. In the regional continuity model, modern Europeans have a direct genetic link to the *Homo erectus* populations that preceded them in Europe. Proponents of this model typically point to continuity and

differences between *Homo erectus* and modern humans in Asia and Europe.

2. The complete replacement theory states that an intrepid line of *Homo sapiens* spread out from Africa and populated the globe starting some 60,000 years ago. In the process, they ultimately replaced *Homo erectus* and all other hominin populations.

3. The partial replacement model adds the element of interbreeding. According to the partial replacement model, modern *Homo sapiens* spread rapidly well beyond the African continent some 60,000 years ago. Along the route they interbred with and eventually replaced all other hominins, including the Neanderthal.

As scientists, anthropologists love new evidence, and that's exactly what they received in 2015 when Beijing paleoanthropologists discovered 47 human teeth in a cave in southern China. The teeth dated to around 100,000 years ago. This discovery puts modern humans in eastern Asia early enough to lend support to the partial replacement model for the peopling of the world.

The Genetic Trail

In addition to fossils, paleoanthropologists also rely on molecular genetics to retrace the global dispersal of humankind. Just as all humans share a common ancestor with all living primates, we also share a much more recent earliest common ancestor with all living *Homo sapiens*.

Geneticists have traced our mtDNA (mitochondrial DNA) and our Y-chromosome DNA back to Africa.

Y-chromosome DNA is genetic material males inherit from their father's line. Y-chromosome Adam is how we refer to the *Homo sapiens* male ancestor that all living humans share. By dating the frequency of human mutations, geneticists estimate that this man lived in Africa, perhaps as early as 100,000 years ago.

Similarly, we've studied mtDNA from across the world in order to determine the woman from whom all modern humans descend. MtDNA is how we genetically explore our maternal inheritance.

●   When a human egg cell is fertilized, chromosomes from

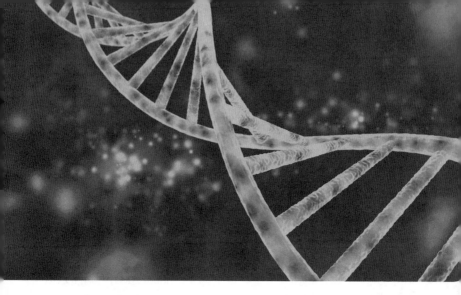

a sperm cell enter the egg and combine with the DNA in the egg's nucleus. The sperm cell's mtDNA, however, never enters the egg, so the fertilized egg retains the mother's exact copy of her mtDNA.

- That's why mtDNA is such an amazing window into our evolutionary past. Based on their analysis of mtDNA from people around the world, scientists estimate that our maternal line as humans dates back to mtEve some 200,000 years ago. Like Y-chromosome Adam, she too would have lived in Africa.

It's important to note the mtEve was not the first *Homo sapiens* woman to walk the Earth. There would have been human women before her and there would have been human women contemporary with her. But it was this particular woman who passed her mitochondria down, through an unbroken female line, to all humans living today.

In any case, as the *Homo sapiens* population grew, they migrated out of Africa and populated the entire planet.

Entering the Americas

For the final segment of this lecture, we'll look at the fossil record, genetics, and climate history to map out the peopling of the Americas.

The Last Glacial Maximum covered continents with ice sheets as recently as 30,000 years ago, and these ice sheets effectively closed the doors of human migration into Northern Europe and North America. But then, around 20,000 years ago, the ice started melting.

Glacial melting increased sea levels and revealed new opportunities for human expansion. It opened up new routes into North America through Siberia. The glacial melt created coastal and interior corridors abundant in the kind of flora and fauna that enticed human hunters and fishers.

Archaeological evidence supports this. In the northern Yukon, the Bluefish Caves are 3 small caves where early humans butchered animals, perhaps as early as 25,000 years ago. That's major: 25,000 years ago, this site and any population who lived there would have been cut off from the rest of North America by those massive ice sheets. The people who spent time in the Bluefish Caves lived on the edge of these ice sheets, hunting large game like mammoth and caribou.

Similarly, further to the west, on the Siberian side of things, there is a site on the Yana River with hundreds of tools made by mammoth hunting humans who lived there around 27,000 years ago.

There's nothing conclusive that shows human presence in the Americas south of the Yukon before 15,000 to 16,000 years ago, but that changed. It was at Fort Rock Cave in Oregon where archaeology unearthed dozens of prehistoric shoes. Some of these dated to 10,000 years ago. With sea levels down, a new land bridge connected Siberia with Alaska, opening the migration into all of the Americas.

Near Murray Springs, Arizona, researchers uncovered a site where nomadic hunters chased big game like mammoths and bison. The stone tools and fossilized bones date the site to over 12,000 years ago, and it's one the earliest human sites in the Americans below Beringia and the Yukon.

Another early site exists at Monte Verde, Chile, where archaeologists found foraged plants, plenty of tools, a hearth, and even some simple animal skin tents with poles. This site dates to 12,500 years ago.

The Clovis Point

Remarkably, most of the people who first settled in the Americas shared a similar tool kit featuring a fluted stone tool called a Clovis point. It's about 2 fingers wide and shorter than a pencil.

In 1932, the archaeologist Edgar Howard came to Clovis, New Mexico. He'd caught word that a local road crew had uncovered unknown quantities of ancient bones. He excavated the site and discovered layers and layers of mammoth bones. Between the bones were seemingly countless specialized spearheads that early Americans had skillfully manufactured for big-game hunting.

Clovis points had amazingly sharp edges that were fluted at the end. Knappers shaped these distinctive lance-like points and would insert them into spears and shafts. People used Clovis points to settle areas from the Pacific Northwest, the American South, and into the Great Lakes. Since that first discovery back in New Mexico, we've now found thousands of Clovis points all across North America.

Genetics

An exciting 21st-century discovery was a comprehensive study of the prehistoric Native American genome. A group of UC Berkeley researchers sequenced the genome of 23 ancient humans found in North and South America, including the DNA of a 12,600 year old boy who was buried in Montana with over 125 artifacts.

Scientists compared these ancient genomes with the genomes of 31 living Native Americans, Pacific Islanders, and Siberians. The results are astounding. They show us that these early Americans share DNA markers with living 21st-century Native Americans, as well as with people from the Pacific Islands and Siberia.

Moreover, this consequential study clears up 2 enduring questions about the first Americans:

1. The first Americans arrived through Siberia after the last ice age was drawing to a close around 20,000 years ago.
2. This population remained in the north for several thousand

Clovis point

years before splitting into northern and southern branches.

The waves of humans coming into the Americas had to wait until the ice barrier melted down, just about 15,000 years ago. That is the same time frame as the documented entry of humans beyond the Yukon.

Anthropologists always remain open to new discoveries, and there is certainly a chance that, in the future, they may discover earlier, pre-Clovis sites in the Americas. Anthropologists may very well find evidence for human migration outside of the Beringian model.

Suggested Reading

Graf, Ketron, and Waters, eds., *Paleoamerican Odyssey*.

Harari, *Sapiens*. New York: Harper, 2015.

Stringer, *Lone Survivors*.

Questions to Consider

1. How does archaeology help us determine when humans first arrived in the Americas? How and when did they arrive?

2. What role did climate play in the peopling of the Americas?

Anthropology and the Question of Race

S
o far in this course, we've seen some of the remarkable ways anthropologists explore the origins and diversity of humankind. And if there's one thing we've learned, it's that our genetics, our biology, and even the archaeological record all converge on one anthropological truth: Despite our physical and cultural differences, we are a single human race. Yet enduring ambiguities remain between race, skin color, and biology. This lecture aims to unpack those while acknowledging that anthropologists, archaeologists included, have had much trouble coming to terms with the concept of race.

Social Darwinism

In the early days of anthropology, Darwin's ideas about the biology of evolution proved so convincing that many leading thinkers of the time started applying this idea far beyond biology. Folks like Herbert Spencer argued that just as biological organisms evolve from simple, single-cell organisms to more complex ones, human cultures evolve from simple societies to highly complex ones.

Their assertion was clear: humans evolve culturally from savage to civilized. This idea of social evolution, or social Darwinism as Spencer described it, became a popular explanation for the diversity of humankind across the globe.

Darwin's book came out in the mid-1800s. As the close of the trans-Atlantic slave trade transitioned into the dawn of European empires, people in Darwin's age were exposed to new and diverse world cultures.

Inspired by Darwin's ideas on biological evolution, social Darwinists used evolution as a way to explain human diversity and to classify people and cultures across the globe. Humans who lived in small, simple societies (like a single-cell organism) were deemed "less evolved" than those who lived in large, complex ones.

As the scientific community ushered in the idea of social Darwinism, the idea spread because it helped make sense of the seemingly limitless human diversity on our planet. Suddenly it became easy to explain why some people were entering the so-called modern world, with industrial factories, powerful trains, and upper-class values, while others were stuck in the past.

The idea of race emerged as an all-encompassing way to describe these vast human differences. The differences Europeans saw in humans from Africa or Asia were attributed to the fact that we all come from distinct lineages which we called races.

Upon reflection, many thinkers further developed this idea of human races, to the extreme that proponents of this way of thinking coined and used the term "white man's burden" to describe the idea that white men had the moral obligation to use their advanced state to uplift non-whites the world over. The concept of the white man's burden was used to justify the colonization of the non-white world.

In 1896, the US Supreme Court heard the case *Plessy v. Ferguson*, in which the justices considered whether the Constitution allowed for discrimination based on white versus non-white races. In a 7-to-1 ruling, the court held that if nature created people and races that were not equal, the Constitution could do nothing to change that.

Eugenics

With millions of dollars of support from wealthy families and foundations, special research centers were built to find solutions to the white man's burden. In 1904, for example, the Station for Experimental Evolution (SEE) was established at Cold Spring Harbor on Long Island.

Researchers at this institute were charged with identifying ways to prevent defective germ plasm, supposedly the biological and primitive remnants of our savage past, from spreading any further.

The researchers at SEE not only developed a series of recommendations on how to proceed with this project, they also started to identify family lines in the area that were tainted by criminality, mental disorders, and physical deformities. The idea was simple: Find a way to limit the reproduction of what they deemed to be defective human germ plasm.

Shockingly, their official recommendations included lethal chambers as the most effective solution, but they advised policy makers and others that the US population was not ready to accept this approach. Instead, other strategies were unleashed, namely marriage and sterilization laws. In 1907, for example, the state of Indiana enacted sterilization laws to make sure criminals and other undesirables could not pass on their defective humanity to another generation.

In 1927, the Supreme Court upheld a Virginia statute that promoted compulsory sterilization of the so-called unfit.

The idea of applying eugenics to improve humankind spread far beyond US borders, and was embraced by many, including Adolf Hitler and his Nazi party. In fact, when Nazi war criminals were tried in Nuremburg, they actually cited the words of US eugenics leaders and Chief Justice Oliver Wendell Holmes to defend their genocidal actions.

Chief Justice Holmes's words from the majority opinion in the aforementioned 1927 case demonstrate how pervasive and public these ideas were. Holmes wrote: "It is better for all the world, if instead of waiting to execute degenerate offspring for crime, or to let them starve for their imbecility, society can prevent those who are manifestly unfit from continuing their kind."

Fortunately, Holmes's perspective and the eugenics project in general began to lose ground in the US in the 1930s and '40s. But this was precisely the time when Nazi Germany was slaughtering millions of Jews, homosexuals, and anyone else they viewed as undesirable.

Franz Boas

Apart from eugenics scholars, there were other science-minded people who took another approach towards exploring and understanding human diversity. The father of American anthropology, a Polish immigrant named Franz Boas, is a great example.

Boas didn't see culture as the product of our biology. Instead, he looked to see how one's environment shapes unique cultural traditions. Because he looked beyond biology to explain human diversity, he argued that there wasn't really a scientific basis for ranking people and cultures on the spectrum of primitive to civilized.

For example, rather than ethnocentrically judging Arctic igloo dwellers as primitive hunter-gatherers, Boas saw them as uniquely adapted to a challenging environment. Ultimately, Boas learned and taught that cultures are neither able to be ranked nor biologically based. They're relative, and as such people from different cultural traditions are equally and fully human. This idea is basically what we call cultural relativity. Some cultures aren't better or worse than others; they're just different.

Franz Boas saw Arctic igloo dwellers as uniquely adapted to a challenging environment.

Theories

When biological determinists saw people who looked different and lived differently from themselves, they ascribed the difference to biology. And as such, they divided humanity into biological races. For example, 18th- and early 19th-century anthropologists who advocated this position commonly described our human origins and races in 1 of 2 ways:

1. Some argued that Africans, Asians, and Europeans (for example) each had distinct origins: multiple Edens, so to speak.

2. Others theorized that despite the fact that humanity shares common origins, humankind split into multiple, biological races like the ones we see listed in the US Census.

The human genome and our knowledge of our hominin ancestors definitively refute both of these theories.

The Myth of Race

If anthropologic evidence tells us that different skin colors and cultures are manifestations of a single biological race, why does the myth of multiple human races persist?

One reason is clumsy use of the term *race*. The myth of multiple races endures in universities, for example: Financial aid and admission applications still use multiple racial categories.

Toward the end of the 20th century, for example, members of the America Anthropological Association gasped with incredulity at the argument put forth by Richard Herrnstein (a psychologist) and his coauthor Charles Murray (a political scientist) in their book *The Bell Curve*.

The controversial authors looked at both genetic and environmental influences on human diversity. The controversial authors ultimately argued that, compared with black Americans, both East Asians and white Americans historically performed better on IQ tests because of their biology—their genetic heritage.

Critics and supporters of this argument fiercely debated these findings. Mel Konner from Emory University, who is a Harvard-trained M.D. as well as an anthropology Ph.D., effectively described why anthropologists and others like Noam Chomsky and Stephen Jay Gould fervently refuted *The Bell Curve's* conclusions. Specifically, he said that Murray and Herrnstein presented strong evidence that genes play a role in intelligence, but their evidence in no way supported their theory that genetics explain the documented differences between the IQs of black and white Americans.

Similarly, in 1994, the members of the AAA put forth an official statement on race to clear up the pervasive myth of multiple biological races. Simply put, they said that all humans are members of a single species, *Homo sapiens*. In their words, "Differentiating species into biologically defined races has proven meaningless and unscientific as a way of explaining human variation."

Health Questions

If racial categories are social constructions, not natural divisions in the human species, then how do anthropologists explain the existence of pervasive health inequalities that affect some groups more than others? For example, why do 40% or more of African Americans have hypertension, when only roughly 30% of non-Hispanic whites are afflicted with this condition?

The anthropologist Clarence Gravlee has an answer. In his well-cited article titled "How Race Becomes Biology: Embodiment of Social Inequality," Gravlee shows that race, despite being a social construction, is very real in terms socioeconomic and health outcomes. Those health outcomes, good or bad, are passed on through the generations.

Gravlee shows that an individual's exposure to racism over a lifetime actually increases one's risk of infant mortality, diabetes, stroke, and high blood pressure, not to mention lower life expectancy. All of these individual health outcomes can impact future generations because any one of them can adversely impact both prenatal and postnatal development and health. Keep in mind that this is the biology of racism rather than the biology of race.

Suggested Reading

Baker, *From Savage to Negro*.

Black, *War against the Weak*.

Jablonski, *Living Color*.

Questions to Consider

1. How has anthropology revised its understanding of race since the late 19th century?

2. To what extent, if any, can socially constructed races become biological?

Archaeology and Human Tools

I n the deep past, the hominin family tree had many branches. This lecture looks at the factors that helped *Homo sapiens* remain the sole remaining survivor on that family tree. Specifically, the lecture turns to archaeology to dig up some answers. First, we'll clear up what archaeologists actually do, and then we'll visit a few archaeological sites to see how the creation of tools is one of the reasons humans are the sole survivors.

What Archaeology Does

Archaeology can not only tell us a lot about when and where humans have lived, but it can also tell us wonderfully curious details about how humans lived. Archaeologists try and figure out what humans were up to, long after they're gone. An archaeologist tracks down, classifies, and analyzes the material remains of people who are no longer present to speak for themselves.

By analyzing these material remains, we learn not only about the daily lives of our ancestors, but also about how humans adapted over the years on the path to our sole-survivor status.

Experimental Archaeology

There are many specializations in archaeology, but 3 are especially relevant to this lecture: experimental archaeology, underwater archaeology, and cultural resource management.

Experimental archaeologists not only explore and interpret the archaeological record, but they recreate the technology and tools of their research populations to probe their lives and minds.

Polynesia provides an excellent example of experimental archaeology. While living on a remote Polynesian island with his wife, the explorer Thor Heyerdahl researched regional cultural traditions as well as the local flora and fauna. He eventually turned his gaze toward human migration and became engrossed in exploring the possibility of human contact between pre-Columbian Polynesian and American populations.

Heyerdahl set out to test his theory that the earliest Americans were in contact with Polynesian groups over 1000 years ago. In 1947, he built a balsa raft and set sail from Peru with Polynesia as his destination.

The journey started in late April. Some 3.5 months and over 4000 miles later, their raft, the *Kon-Tiki*, reached the Tuamotu Islands in French Polynesia. This remarkable journey doesn't prove definitively that ancient Peruvians visited the Polynesian Islands, but it does show us that pre-Columbian contact between South Americans and Polynesians is entirely plausible. Humans could have, technically speaking, made it from Peru to Polynesia without modern equipment or materials.

Underwater Archaeology

Over 70% of the earth's surface is covered in water. If archaeologists are going to search for traces of humanity in every nook and corner of the world, some of them better look beneath the surface of the sea. That's where underwater archaeology comes in.

One exciting example of underwater archaeology research is the recovery and preservation of shipwrecks. Just off the coast of Beaufort, NC for example, is the site where researchers discovered the pirate Blackbeard's flagship, *Queen Anne's Revenge*.

Besides navigation equipment, cannons, guns, and gold, archaeologists also unearthed kitchen utensils and personal possessions like game pieces and smoking pipes, all of which help us reconstruct what life was like for sailors in the early 1700s.

Interestingly, Blackbeard's ship doctors dealt with everything

from bullet wounds and dysentery to scurvy and burns. The ship's medical gear included measuring devices as well as a mortar and pestle for mixing up medicine. There were even a clyster pump for delivering enemas and a mercury syringe for treating syphilis.

Cultural Resource Management

This lecture's 3rd example of archaeological work is cultural resource management. The idea of cultural resource management is an intentional parallel to natural resource management. Just as scientists preserve and study natural resources, some archaeologists apply their talents to preserving, studying, and sharing a wide variety of cultural resources.

For the Tennessee Valley Authority, as a large-scale example, cultural resource management included the management of over 9,000 archaeological sites, the relocation of cemeteries, and collaborative research and management of cultural resources on Native American lands.

Another example of cultural resource management work takes us to the Nashville Sounds baseball stadium on the banks of the Cumberland River. Because the stadium was built in an area known for artifacts from early Native American settlements, cultural resource management archaeologists were on the scene to facilitate excavations and ensure that important archaeological artifacts were not destroyed or disturbed by the construction process.

Tool Making

Next, this lecture will visit some archaeological sites to dig up the early history of human tool making. Its first destination is a dried-up riverbed in Kenya. That's where, in 2011 and 2012, anthropologists discovered the oldest hominin tools ever found. They found over 100 artifacts that show us that upright apes, or hominins, were making tools over 3 million years ago.

The next oldest tool unearthed dates to 2.6 million years ago, and was found in neighboring Ethiopia. This tool style, which we call the Oldowan toolkit, is a very early type of a manufactured stone tool that was widely adopted by our hominin ancestors. Archaeologists and paleoanthropologists have found Oldowan tools throughout east Africa and all the way down into southern Africa.

And they also found, in these Oldowan sites, clear use of fire. Our *Homo habilis* ancestors were quick to develop and adopt Oldowan tool production as part of their survival strategy. Oldowan tools opened up new ways of preparing meals. In general, the Oldowan tool style is known as a chopper. It had a single intentionally crafted blade, which was perfect for butchering.

Acheulean Handaxe

This lecture's next destination is a site named Saint-Acheul in northern France. That is where, in 1847, researchers discovered fossil evidence of the next great leap forward in tool making. This new tool type, now referred to as the Acheulean style, has been found in southern Africa, across east Africa, into the Mediterranean world, southern Europe, and Asia.

With its revolutionary design, the Achulean tradition produced an all-in-one household gadget that slices,

Stone axe head

dices, chops, grinds, cracks, digs, and more. These handaxes were slightly larger than the Oldowan tools they came to replace in the archaeological record. Uniquely, they had a signature teardrop shape, and they were symmetrically crafted on both sides.

Acheulean tool making essentially emerged with the arrival of *Homo erectus*. Confirming the *Homo erectus* connection, archaeologists discovered Achuelan tools in Africa that date back to well over 1.5 million years ago, and then slightly after that in Asia and into Europe.

The Microlith

As knappers (or tool makers) became more specialized, they became experts at selecting and shaping the best materials into a remarkable toolkit. In the beginning of the Acheulean tradition, knappers started with what is called a core stone.

Then, they used a hammer stone to chip away at the stone tool they pictured in their mind. Over time, knappers found more and more uses for the sharp flakes that splintered off from the core stone during the crafting of a large handaxe. The archaeological record shows that knappers were clearly in the business of making core stone tools AND flake tools just as *Homo sapiens* emerged in the fossil record some 200,000 years ago.

One last major technique in stone tools burst into the archaeological record around 12,000 years ago. As glaciers melted and sea levels rose, humans were releasing their newest stone technology: the microlith.

The Northern Hemisphere was covered in ice for about 1.5 million years. Our ancestors created tools for cooperatively hunting and processing the huge mammoth and other big game that roamed the earth during the Paleolithic era.

But, after 1.5 million years, the ice age drew to a close. And melting ice sheets and rising sea levels weren't the only changes humans were going to have to get used to. As landscapes dramatically transformed from tundra to forests, savannahs, and mountains, the animal population changed too.

The big game followed the path into extinction. Humans needed a new toolkit to chase the more plentiful, yet smaller and flighty, prey like deer, boar, and rabbits.

Microliths answered this need. These small stone tools were made of flint or chert, another sedimentary rock. Highly skilled knappers manufactured points that were less than a centimeter wide.

By making an array of very small stone tools that could be affixed to arrows and spears, Mesolithic humans effectively transitioned out of the ice age and into a radically new world. In other words, we see once more how tool making allowed us to adapt to our environment, embolden our food system, and sustain our ongoing survival.

Suggested Reading

Fagan, *Ancient Lives*.

Henrich, *The Secret of Our Success*.

Waters and Jennings, *The Hogeye Clovis Cache*.

Questions to Consider

1. What is experimental archaeology, and how is it different from other specializations in archaeology?

2. What are some of the oldest tools on Earth, and how does the history of stone tools help us retell the geographic and temporal history of humankind?

Agricultural Roots of Civilization

P aleoanthropologists and archaeologists analyze the fossil record to
reveal the myriad ways humans have cooperated to produce food
across the millennia. That fossil record definitively tells us that our
human ancestors were hunter-gatherers, of one variation or another, for
99.98% of our 7,000,000-year history. Even if we reduce the scope of our
family tree to only modern humans—otherwise known as *Homo sapiens*—
we've been hunter-gatherers for about 190,000 of the past 200,000 years.
As odd as it may sound, farming, in the grand scheme of things, is about
as modern as space travel and the Internet. This lecture looks at how
agriculture came to be.

The Pre-Agricultural Past

At first thought, the idea of living a migratory, hunter-gatherer lifestyle might sound like a horrifying alternative to those of us who rely on modern ubiquities like carryout and grocery stores.

However, as renowned anthropologist Marshall Sahlins explains, the hunter-gatherer lifestyle had surprising advantages. Hunter-gatherer societies—which consisted of small, close-knit bands of fewer than 100 people—lived prosperously, had diverse and balanced diets, and even had longer and healthier lifespans than early farmers.

What's more, the small size of their bands made their communities adaptive and manageable. These small societies were decentralized and actually rather egalitarian with respect to leadership, work, and social class. Additionally, these small communities were migratory, which allowed them to go where the food was.

The gradual shift to agriculture was thousands of years in the making, and it emerged in different places at different times.

Parietal Art, Grinding Stones, and Genetics

We don't have histories recording the shift to agriculture written by our earliest farming ancestors, but we do have strong historical evidence. For example, in the mountains of southwest Libya, rock art—which anthropologists refer to as parietal art—documents that the regional domestication of cattle was well established some 7,000 years ago.

At the Tin Newen site, for example, early humans recorded all kinds of daily activities in their parietal art. We see thoughtful paintings of lots of cattle tended by a few human figures here and there. Further down the line is a scene of people seated in small groups like a prehistoric café.

Archaeologists have also analyzed pottery fragments and fossilized bones from the region to further substantiate this transition from foraging to agriculture and animal husbandry.

In Asia, the archaeologist Li Liu has provided another compelling regional example of how anthropologists date the origins of farming. When Liu analyzed grinding stones from a site near China's Yellow River, she found that they dated back some 23,000 years— not too far on the timeline from the coming domestication of plants.

Starch analysis and other techniques show us that for thousands of years, people in this region processed foraged foods like grasses, roots, and wild millet seed. Generations of these foraging activities gradually ushered in the domestication of wild plants like millet, which became a staple for ancient Chinese civilization.

Archaeologists have unearthed evidence that people in the Near East were growing cereals and figs as early as 12,000 years ago. In Mexico around the same time, people were growing squash and playing with teosinte, the wild version of maize. Meanwhile in China, we see the emergence of rice cultivation.

Genetics also helps us date the domestication of animals like cattle and goats. This dates to roughly the same timeframe, just a little before we begin to see archaeological evidence of farming.

Why Farm?

The agricultural transformation was a widespread response to the changing ecological, technological, biological, and cultural lives of humans. The shift began around 10,000 to 12,000 years ago.

One important factor was we evolved. Hunter-gatherers in the Middle to Late Stone Age were remarkably different from our earliest ancestors. The Middle Stone Age brain, for example, evolved to be 4 times larger than the brains of *Sahelanthropus*—the earliest hominin ancestor, which dates back 6–7 million years.

After millions of years, we became hunting and foraging machines. This led to surplus food, which in turn led to 2 choices: Build granaries for the surplus, or build permanent or semi-permanent settlements at the most productive hunting and foraging sites. Our pre-agricultural ancestors did both.

Progressively more hunter-gatherer populations began to like the idea of settling down occasionally to generate and store surplus food, tools, and all the other things that don't fit into a migrant's backpack.

Climate Change

Another major factor that accelerated our transition to agriculture was climate change. After the most recent ice age peaked around 20,000 years ago, humans watched their hunter-gatherer worlds change dramatically.

If we return to parietal art, our southeastern Algerian ancestors left us rock paintings depicting the Sahara as a lush, grassy expanse with giraffes, elephants, trees, streams, and lakes.

Animal bones and geological evidence confirm the Sahara was green as recently as 8,000 years ago.

Then, increased temperatures and humidity progressively dried up the once lush Sahara. Along major rivers like the Euphrates and Tigris, these changes created ideal conditions for the rise of agriculture.

Similar climatic pressures challenged pre-agricultural societies across the globe, and over the generations, humans gradually changed the way they made food. They became farmers.

Farming, Families, and Breakthroughs

Sedentary, agriculture-based living made it much easier to raise children. Raising an infant is exhausting enough—even in the 21st century and even with the very best baby monitors, diaper stations, and cribs. But imagine how hard parenting would be if we were all migratory foragers.

It's no surprise that when folks settled down and started farming, their populations grew. Now capable of generating some serious food surplus, human societies eventually grew into massive ancient civilizations in China, Egypt, Peru, and all over the world.

In short, the transition to agriculture inspired sedentary living and urban centers, and it sparked technological breakthroughs like writing, mathematics, medicine and much more.

But this shift wasn't an easy one. In his classic text, *Paleopathology at the Origins of Agriculture,* George Armelagos analyzes fossilized human remains to document early-agricultural diseases.

He found evidence that early farmers in the Illinois River Valley, when compared with the hunter-gatherers who preceded them, were rather stressed out and sickly: They had bone lesions, anemia, degenerative spinal conditions, and even lower life expectancy.

Despite these poor health outcomes, the relatively rapid spread of farming indicates that agriculture was a rather seductive alternative to hunter-gatherer life.

Poverty and Wealth

One more significant change was spurred by agricultural life: the emergence of poverty and wealth.

Today's tech geniuses reap benefits from the gadgets and patents they create, and that incentivized system was in effect for early farmers too. Super-farmers could become extremely rich.

Yet, for all its glitz and glory, farming was a very risky food production strategy. A single pest infestation, inadequate rainfall, or a loose group of cattle could all ruin a farming family or community in a flash.

We see this in parts of the world even today. For example, in Mali, a family endured several years of debt and scarcity only because one of their best farmers broke his leg.

Society tasked scientists with this next food revolution. Organized into national and international research institutes, funded by government and industry, and aligned with university research programs, agricultural scientists sought solutions to the feed the planet.

The Green Revolution

An existential food crisis emerged in the 20th century, and here in the 21st century, we're not past it just yet.

Thomas Malthus

Prior to the 20th century, scholars like Thomas Malthus warned that exponential population growth would eventually outstrip food production. As a result, Malthus warned of a future of famines and disease.

Nearly 2 centuries after Malthus voiced his concerns, fears of runaway population growth destroying humanity found a new voice in Paul and Anne Ehrlich's classic, *The Population Bomb*. This influential 1968 book predicted that widespread starvation was imminent, barring another food revolution.

In the US, for example, cereal farmers used scientists' improved seed, and the results were indeed revolutionary. By the start of the 21st century, US farmers more than tripled their cereal yields.

Early on, the 20th-century food revolution was optimistically named the Green Revolution. Farmers hoping to reap improved Green Revolution harvests had to change the way they farmed. For instance, they had to stop producing their own seed on the farm. Instead, they had to begin buying improved seed engineered by agricultural specialists.

After buying modified seed, farmers also needed to buy fertilizer, pesticide, herbicide, seed treatment, and so on. These petroleum-based products fueled the Green Revolution.

Unfortunately, as we settle further into the 21st century, many of the world's farmers, including the poorest of the poor, have yet to reap Green Revolution benefits like improved yields.

Green Revolution farming has benefited some more than others. Sub-Saharan African farmers, for example, grew only 1 ton of cereal per hectare in the 1960s, while US farmers harvested 2 tons per hectare.

To this day, in places like Mali, family farmers still get an optimistic average of around 1 ton of grain per hectare. Conversely, US cereal producers have harvested a stunning 6–7 tons per hectare since the early 1990s.

As extreme hunger and food insecurity persist into yet another century, humanity is again turning to scientists and other specialists in search of the future of food. Like the early humans who brought us agriculture, today's society is faced with its own set of unique challenges, including population growth, climate change, and global security.

Suggested Reading

Cleveland, *Balancing on a Planet*.

Cohen and Armelagos, *Paleopathology at the Origins of Agriculture*.

Shostak, *Nisa*.

Questions to Consider

1. When and why did humans start farming, and how did this agricultural transformation alter the human experience?

2. In what ways is the planting of seeds also a planting of civilization?

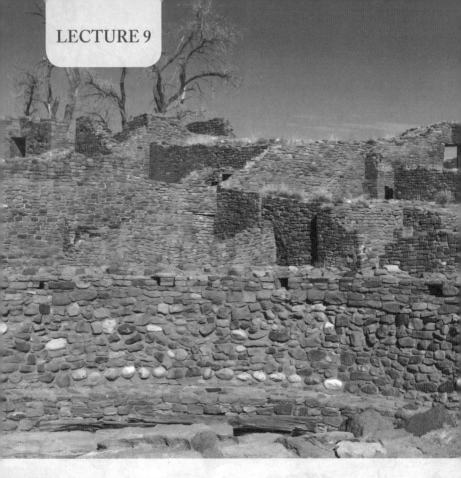

Rise of Urban Centers

I n previous lectures, we saw how tool making and agriculture helped
early humans adapt and endure as a species. This lecture continues
our archaeological exploration by showing how our human ancestors
invested in the future of humankind by building major cities and
civilizations across the planet. To start, we'll take a moment to check out the
earliest known cities on record, and then our archaeological adventure will
give us an in-depth look at a few astonishing early, world-class cities that
forever shaped the story of humankind.

Criteria for a City

What are the criteria for a city being considered as such? The influential archaeologist Gordon Childe gives us a checklist we can use, albeit loosely, to identify early cities across the archaeological record:

1. A city has a large, dense population with long-distance trade.
2. A city exists as a class-structured society.
3. A city has some system of governance and taxation.
4. A city boasts cultural resources including artwork, monuments, scientific knowledge, and the arts.

The actual emergence of anything resembling a city didn't occur until around 12,000 years ago. Anthropologists who study the emergence of cities generally note that humans started urbanizing several thousand years after the most recent ice age ended.

Ancient Mesopotamia

Archaeologists point to ancient Mesopotamia as the site of the first known urban revolution in the history of humankind. Mesopotamia is the ancient region between the Tigris and Euphrates rivers. There, in the 4th millennium B.C.E., a revolution began that would give rise to such powerful cities as Ur, Babylon, and Nineveh.

Jericho also fits the bill for one of the first human cities on record. With its 6-foot-wide protective walls, Jericho has been home to at least 20 unique settlements, the earliest dating back over 10,000 years ago. But it took another millennium before the droughts and cold conditions in the region gave way to more fertile grounds for the first cities.

With better conditions and an abundant ecology, people settled into permanent settlements and farming. One of the most remarkable archaeological discoveries of early Jericho life is the clear evidence for religious or cultural practices dealing with funerary practices.

The early urban Jericho people tended to bury their dead under the floors of their small, circular, clay houses. Remarkably, they occasionally preserved the heads

Ruins in Jericho

of the deceased, plastering the skull to preserve a rather lifelike, albeit spooky, appearance.

Jericho is more familiar to us than many other first cities because of its prominence in the Bible. The site is in the modern-day West Bank, about 15 miles northeast of Jerusalem. Archaeologists think people were attracted to the region because of its proximity to the Jordan River and its plentiful springs and palm trees.

Upward of 3,000 people lived in these earliest versions of Jericho, and they helped usher in the agricultural transformation with domesticated barley and wheat production.

Byblos

Well before Egypt started building pyramids, ancient seafaring Phoenicians built Gebal, a small fishing community. By 3000 B.C.E., Gebal had grown into a full-fledged city called Byblos, another one of the first cities on record.

Byblos was ideally situated for the development of agriculture and international trade. It ushered in the powerful ancient Phoenician civilization and played a pivotal role in the development of the written word.

The archaeological record traces the early development of the Phoenician alphabet to Byblos. That ancient Phoenician alphabet is connected to languages the world over. English speakers, for example, have no trouble identifying a Phoenician L, M, or N. Even the K is just a rotated version of what we use today.

network of *hammams*, which were essentially a massive bathing infrastructure.

Sadly, like untold numbers of ancient cities, Aleppo has endured colossal tragedy and destruction into the 21st century. The civil war in Syria, which began in 2011, has wreaked havoc upon the people and the architecture of Aleppo, imperiling one of humanity's first major cities.

Aleppo

Aleppo is an ancient city that remains a major urban center in contemporary Syria. Aleppo, once a powerful geopolitical neighbor to pharaonic Egypt, dates back 8,000 years.

The region's archaeology shows us that nomadic camps roamed through the region as far back as 12,000 to 13,000 years ago. That's right at the cusp of the Neolithic transition from hunting and gathering to settled societies.

Aleppo eventually grew into a world city known for its legendary citadel, fortified palaces, impressively ornate mosques, and an extensive

Uruk

Some 5,000 years ago, ancient Uruk was a city on the Euphrates River, with a population of over 50,000 people. It was located about 150 miles south of modern Baghdad.

After the Euphrates River branched out some 10,000 years ago, the early inhabitants of the region built adobe-style houses near the river, attracted and sustained by the abundant ecosystem.

The region's natural resources inspired these early populations toward agricultural innovation, and they eventually built complex irrigation systems and canals, which helped transform this settlement into one of Mesopotamia's earliest and most famous world cities.

Uruk is also the scene of one of the greatest ancient literary works of all time: the *Epic of Gilgamesh*. Here's a synopsis:

- In the earliest of days, Uruk was ruled by a rather mean king: Gilgamesh. His reign of terror was so brutal that the people of Uruk prayed to the gods in hopes of peace.
- The gods heard their prayers and came up with a solution: They sent a primitive man to earth named Enkidu. He set out to defeat Gilgamesh, but befriended him instead.
- But then Enkidu died. His death crushed the king, who set out to seek Utnapishtim, the holder of the secret to eternal life.
- As it turns out, Utnapishtim was rewarded with immortality from a god named Enlil. It seems Enlil gave the gift of immortality for Utnapishtim's heroic effort of building an ark to preserve his family and all kinds of wild animals.
- As Gilgamesh left Utnapishtim to return to his kingdom back

in Uruk, Utnapishtim took pity on Gilgamesh, and he shared one last secret. He reveals that there is a sacred plant at the bottom of the sea that could restore his youth.

- Gilgamesh goes underwater to retrieve the miracle plant. Despite having the source of immortality in his hands, he loses it moments later as he's bathing.
- With that final loss, Gilgamesh returns to his kingdom, where he is pleased by the remarkable wall his subjects have built to protect all of Uruk.

Stories like these may contain plenty of wonderfully magical and unrealistic elements, but they also contain fragments of the ancient Uruk worldview. Beyond interpretivist analyses of plot and characters, the content within the Gilgamesh story reveals hints about local ecology, values, and artistic or symbolic expression.

For example, in 2015, researchers at the Sulaymaniyah Museum discovered a new segment of the Gilgamesh adventure. This new morsel takes Gilgamesh and his pal Enkidu into a cedar forest where they meet up with monkeys and birds before they kill a demigod. It offers what we might otherwise consider to be an environmental morality tale.

In Uruk, the people developed both numbers and writing symbols. Archaeologists estimate that it took about 1000 years to go from scraping pictures in clay to a complex writing system that allowed for the composition of epic tales like the adventures of King Gilgamesh.

As the earliest settlers in the region gradually built sedentary lives and agricultural surplus, temples became some of the original sites for redistributing surplus food. As warfare among Mesopotamian city-states proliferated in the age of metals, religious power bases conveniently shared their surplus with warlords and others who had the capacity to protect Uruk from attackers.

Gilgamesh

Tiwanaku

The rise of cities was a global phenomenon. In modern-day Bolivia, not far from the shores of Lake Titicaca, are the remains of ancient Tiwanaku. Just over 2,000 years ago, the settlers at Tiwanaku were on track to building one of the most historic cities in South America.

From around 400 to 1100 C.E., Tiwanaku was a thriving capital city with adobe homes and a massive ceremonial complex with temples, pyramids, palaces, and brilliant archaeological monuments.

One of the most impressive monuments is the Gate of the Sun, which is a massive stone cut into an open gateway covered in intricate carvings. At the top is a great bas-relief image of a god wearing an imposing headdress. Remarkably, archaeologists have interpreted the complex pattern of these carved images as a farming calendar.

Another Tiwanaku feat was their underground water drainage system, and an absolutely brilliant network of irrigation canals that made Tiwanaku an agricultural powerhouse. They built a network of canals around some 50,000 raised bed fields to feed an entire empire.

This wasn't just about delivering water to plants. These raised beds also naturally protected crops from frost damage, a serious problem for Andean farmers.

Here's how it works: Water in the canals surrounds these raised beds, and it soaks the grounded roots, providing a steady source of water. But as the day goes on, the Sun heats the canal water as well.

When the cold mountain evening draws in the frost, the warm water releases its heat as a misty vapor

Tiwanaku, Bolivia

that literally covers the raised beds like a blanket protecting the delicate plants.

The symbolic, artistic, architectural, and agricultural legacy of this Tiwanaku was confirmed and celebrated in 2015. The occasion: After winning his 3rd term as president of Bolivia, Evo Morales invited the world back to the Sun Gate and the Tiwanaku ruins as the site of his inauguration.

As the country's first indigenous president, his success and his Tiwanaku inauguration help reclaim the glory of this ancient city as a striking metaphor for the ingenuity and power of Bolivians.

Suggested Reading

Jennings, *Killing Civilization*.

Leick, *Mesopotamia*.

Pauketat, *Cahokia*.

Questions to Consider

1. Where and when did some of the earliest known human cities emerge?

2. When and why did humans begin to create cities?

3. Why did ancient cities fall? Were there similarities in the conditions that led to their decline?

Anthropological Perspectives on Money

The past few lectures have introduced some of the game-changing things that humans did to become the sole remaining hominins. For example, we've seen how agriculture enabled humans to develop food surpluses and to transition to a sedentary lifestyle, which itself promoted a population explosion. And we've seen how the emergence of cities provided humans with opportunities to make remarkable strides culturally and technologically. This lecture looks at how we created numbers and money.

Numbers

Generally speaking, there are 3 phases to the creation of human numbers. First, biological anthropology teaches us about rudimentary number sense. Next comes the development of the early number concept. Finally, we get to counting with actual numbers.

The rudimentary number sense is phase 1, and it's not exclusive to humans. Other animals display rudimentary number sense too, and we humans still have it today. Rudimentary number sense doesn't use quantities. It's about sensing less or more—relative amounts.

An excellent example of rudimentary number sense is the solitary wasp. One type, the *Eumenes*, is sexually dimorphic; females are much larger than males. Remarkably, the mother wasp provides her developing larvae with food, usually small grubs.

The wasp provides exactly 10 grubs for each female larva. They provide half as many grubs per male larva. The wasp is not counting up from 1 to 5 and 10. It just knows 5 and 10. The wasp has rudimentary numbers sense.

The 2nd phase that leads to actual numbers as we understand them today is the early number concept. Think of this as a midpoint between modern numbers and rudimentary number sense. In this phase, we use clever devices and terms to get specific quantities.

An example: In the Andes Mountains, proto-accountants used a system of strings and knots called quipus to record important numbers like debts or annual harvests. Archaeological iconography and artifacts date this system to just under 5000 years ago.

Once agriculture seeded cities and empires, civilizations across the globe created number systems. From the Maya and Egyptians to the Chinese dynasties, numbers themselves appear to be as invaluable as tools and agriculture in terms of sustaining our species.

The Anthropology of Money

When we want to examine the earliest human societies, we largely depend on archaeology to reconstruct the remains of the day into human stories. It's a remarkable process that has taught us volumes about the origins of many early creations.

Two of the biggest names in the anthropology of money aren't archaeologists at all, but when they write about the origins of money, they head straight to the archaeological record. David Graeber's work *Debt: The First 5,000 Years* is perhaps the definitive book on debt, providing an exhaustive history of money and credit since the time of the ancient Sumerians.

And similarly there's Caroline Humphrey's extensive body of work on the history and cultural complexities of bartering. Both of them consult the archaeological record and much more to discover a massive truth that contradicts the traditional idea that bartering led to money, which in turn led to credit.

There never was an exclusively barter-based society, or at least not according to the empirical record. As a matter of fact, everywhere anthropologists have encountered bartering, it has always been in societies that concurrently use money.

Credit

As Graeber notes, the earliest archaeological evidence of financial transactions doesn't show us the money; it shows us debt (and therefore credit). If we go back to the first urban revolution in Mesopotamia, we find some of the absolute oldest financial records ever found. They are cuneiform tablets that recorded credit. Ancient Mesopotamians leaders created something called money of account.

Around 5000 years ago, city dwellers in Mesopotamia had established a fixed exchange rate to settle accrued debts. Citizens could take silver on credit, and then repay the debt with grain.

With a fixed rate set to exchange grains and silver, folks recorded debts on clay tablets, and then at harvest, accounts were settled. This is credit, or technically speaking, it's money of account, and it appears to be the earliest recorded financial transaction between humans. It happened independently in different sites with different materials.

It's suggested that people in early agrarian communities probably took seasonal loans in much the same way that many small-scale family farmers in Africa, Asia, and Latin America do to this day.

Coins

As societies grew, thrived, and interacted, precious metals became cross-cultural and timeless mechanisms to facilitate long-distance and local trade. Metals were more durable than paper or clay, and the fact that they can be scaled by weight and metal type makes it easier to trade, even across regional currencies.

Starting just under 3,000 years ago, evidence starts to show coins and precious metals as actual units of value. Archaeologists have unearthed coins all across Asia and into the Mediterranean.

In Turkey, which was once called Lydia, coins were found dating back to around 600 B.C.E. The Greek historian Herodotus advises us that Lydians were intrepid traders

who bridged Eastern and Western civilizations. As such, it's no surprise that they were early adopters of coin currency. Their currency was called the stater.

We can trace people trading specific weights of gold and silver bars in the names they used to differentiate between various denominations. The 96th denomination of a stater, for example, weighed of the weight of a full stater.

The earliest staters were composed of electrum, which is a naturally occurring alloy of gold and silver. But eventually Lydians modified their system by introducing pure versions of both gold and silver staters. In this new system, it took 10 silver staters to get 1 gold stater.

Paper Money

By the year 1007, the Song dynasty of China was minting over 1 million coins a year. Successful merchants were burdened by success because they had to haul and store all kinds of coins.

As part of the solution, authorities gave exclusive franchises to a few lucky enterprises that became deposit shops. Merchants could deposit money and goods at one of these shops, and they would get a receipt for what they left behind.

First, merchants traded these receipts in a proto-cash transaction. Then, once the central government claimed full control over the deposit system, China effectively produced the world's first paper currency that was issued and backed by a government treasury.

Centuries would pass before paper currencies emerged in Europe. That's exactly why Marco Polo, an anthropologist years before his time, was flabbergasted and inspired by the paper currency used throughout Kublai Khan's empire in the 13th century.

While coins made it to Europe very early, paper money didn't emerge until almost the 1700s, and it wasn't immediately embraced. Instead of paper, Europeans stuck with coins, and in the absence of coins, they used alternative devices like the tally stick.

King Henry I's England, circa 1100 C.E., required subjects to pay

King Henry I of
England

taxes using tally sticks, which
calculated debts and payments in
local currency denominations. The
sticks were segments of branches

or sometimes bones that people
carved and notched to document
a debt or payment.

Alternative Currencies and the Future

Alternative currencies are a fascinating phenomenon in the history of money. We're all familiar with coins and cash, but through the ages, people have also devised a range of alternative currencies. In the days before paper money was common, other money types like cowrie shells, clam beads, and leather sheets were used to facilitate exchange. Local currencies were part of what led to success in the American colonies, and they continue to help communities thrive into the current era.

One modern alternative currency example is the BerkShare of the Berkshire region in Massachusetts. Residents buy 100 BerkShares for $95. Then they spend this money in the community. Recipients can use it as full value at other businesses, or they can cash it in at the local bank for a 5% fee. Remarkably, some 20,000 residents purchased millions and millions of BerkShares from 2006 to 2016.

The history of money includes many different forms of currency. It's not just about coins and cash. And it seems that no single form of currency endures forever. It stands to reason that there are certainly some changes in store for how we use and understand money in the future.

From wearable, touchless payment options to phones, ATM cards, and web payments, our dollars are more virtual than ever. For years and years now, our paychecks have been electronically transferred into our personal accounts.

But ironically, one of the wealthiest empires in the Americas didn't have money. It was the Incas. The Incas had a community labor system in which males 15 and older worked for the state.

These workers collectively built thousands of miles of roads and palaces. They did so with amazing block work. In return for this fairly demanding group labor, the Incan government provided everything from housing and food to clothing.

Without money changing hands, and without markets, Incans collectively fulfilled their basic needs. All the while, they piled up hoards of gold and silver. But it's likely that Incan life was incalculably sweeter for the rulers versus the citizens.

Suggested Reading

Graeber, *Debt*.

Hart, *The Memory Bank*.

Humphrey and Hugh-Jones, *Barter, Exchange, and Value*.

Questions to Consider

1. How does anthropology's explanation for the history of money differ from the history presented in classical economics textbooks? Why?

2. Who were some of the first civilizations to make coins and cash? What did that early money look like?

3. Why do economic anthropologists and others predict the end of money as we know it? What possibly could replace a $100 bill?

Anthropological
Perspectives on Language

This lecture's mission is to explore the development and nature of human language. Like cities, farming, tools, and money, language has definitely played a starring role in our continued survival as a species. The study of language will bring us right back to the primates, but we'll also get our first real glance of the 3rd subfield of anthropology: linguistics.

Tamarin Monkeys

Deep in the rainforests of Central America, primatologists interested in the origins of language record how tamarin monkeys act as well as their vocalizations. Eventually, researchers can start to break their code to see how this monkey talk actually works.

In tamarins, primatologists have already recorded and catalogued almost 40 distinct types of vocalizations. For instance, the greeting chirp is called the B chirp.

Tamarins make other calls too, like whistles. When they combine vocalizations like whistles and chirps, they actually convey simple sentences to their families and friends. For example, they can tell each other that there's a predator around. This is revolutionary: There was a time that we thought communicating in sentences was solely a human trait.

Apes

A handful of apes have helped us explore the boundaries of human versus other ape-to-ape communication.

In the 1930s, Gua was a chimpanzee who lived with Luella and Winthrop Kellogg. The Kelloggs brought home Gua, a 7.5-month-old chimpanzee, to raise him alongside their own 10-month-old son, Donald. This duo spent 12 hours a day together and they were fast friends.

Remarkably, in the year they lived together, Gua actually was a quicker study on basic manual tasks like using a spoon. That said, Gua simply wasn't able to make progress with learning to speak. In fact, after about a year it was Donald who started imitating Gua's sounds. Shortly after that, the Kelloggs returned Gua to a primate research center.

In the late 1940s and into the 1950s, the psychologists Catherine and Keith Hayes tried a similar experiment, raising a young chimpanzee, Viki, as a human. Despite tireless efforts on everyone's part, Viki only learned to speak four words: mama, papa, cup, and up. Sadly, Viki died of viral meningitis at the age of 7.

Another pair of researchers, Allan and Beatrix Gardner, changed the way we think about primates and their linguistic potential. The

Gardners raised a chimpanzee named Washoe as a human, but not with a sibling. To gauge Washoe's linguistic abilities, the Gardners taught her American Sign Language (ASL). In all she learned some 250 words, which she later taught to her adopted chimpanzee son.

The 2nd chimpanzee who learned ASL was named Lucy. Lucy lived her human life with Maurice K. Temerlin. She learned ASL from Roger Fouts, and she was a natural, even displaying humor.

Lucy and Washoe made it clear that our primate cousins have the capacity to learn our human language. More contemporary research has revealed that we are only scratching the surface of the linguistic boundary between humans and the other apes. The famous gorilla Koko, for example, has learned over 1000 ASL signs.

However, the influential linguist Noam Chomsky warns us not to get our hopes up about future conversations with gorillas about the meaning of life. His primary critique is based on the idea that our primate cousins just don't have the unique linguistic legacy developed exclusively in the *Homo*

sapiens line. Their physiology, neurology, bodies, and brains preclude them from any advanced comprehension of human language.

Historical Lingustics

What exactly is human language? That terrific question brings us to linguistics, the 3rd subfield of anthropology. And within that subfield itself, there are 3 major specializations that help us understand the origins and nature of human language:

1. Historical linguistics: the evolution and extinction of language.
2. Descriptive linguistics: the mechanics of language.
3. Sociocultural linguistics: the relationship between language and culture

Historical linguists collectively build a beautiful linguistic tree that shows us how our languages have branched out and spread through various populations across the globe.

One tool that that helps to create our massive human language tree is glottochronology. Just as we can map the spread of humankind into the Americas, we can use glottochronology to map the diversification of human languages across the planet.

The gist of glottochronology is that 2 languages like English and German share linguistic origins, and therefore they still share some core vocabulary words. The longer they are apart, however, the more their core vocabularies will differ.

Linguists and others sometimes question the reliability of glottochronology. More recently, with more sophisticated computational methods, complex phylogenetic reconstructions help us see how languages, like farming and tools, have spread across the planet with intrepid *Homo sapiens*.

In addition to the evolution of language, historical linguistics also researches dead and disappearing languages. It's noting that of the

6,000 to 7,000 languages known today, half or more of these languages are predicted to go extinct by the end of the 21st century.

Many Native American languages—the languages of the Caddo, Menominee, Yuchi, Pawnee, and many other peoples—are endangered because there are only a few speakers left who can keep them alive. There are efforts, though, to improve this situation. For example, the Living Tongues Institute for Endangered Languages works to prevent Native American languages like Yuchi from dying out.

Descriptive Linguistics

The field of descriptive linguistics focuses on the conventions and mechanics that make language work. There are 5 key elements of human language:

1. Phonemes, which are the base sound units with no meaning.
2. Morphemes, which are the base units of meaning, like *un-* or *non-*.
3. Grammar, which covers rules.
4. Syntax, which covers sentence structure.

5. Semantics, which cover meaning

With these constituent pieces, there are limitless possibilities to what we can learn about the nature and origins of language. Linguists working in the Middle East, for example, studied a community named Al-Sayyid, which offers intriguing insights into our instinct for language.

This Bedouin community in Israel's Negev Desert has a large deaf population, the result of a local genetic mutation that leads to a higher prevalence of deafness. This village developed a distinctly local sign language, the Al-Sayyid Bedouin Sign Language, which is structurally distinct from both the spoken languages and the regionally dominant sign languages of Hebrew and Arabic.

Ultimately, the development and evolution of this unique, local sign language supports the idea that humans are born communicators. We're equipped to create languages when we need to.

Sociocultural Linguistics

Sociocultural linguists investigate the relationship between language and culture. Linguistic norms definitely differ across cultures, and those differences can shape the way we observe and perceive our daily lives.

In Mali, for instance, farmers who speak Bamanankan utilize a 24-hour cycle to track each day, but in day-to-day life, they use Bamanankan time categories. These categories are different from Western modes of speech, which tend to focus on specific hours and minutes.

The whole day may fit a 24-hour cycle, but the pacing of work teams, family meals, and daily life is still basically structured into 4, dynamic, unequal parts:

- Phase 1: Waking and starting work.
- Phase 2: A brief break, followed by more work.
- Phase 3: Return to the household for showers and tea.
- Phase 4: Eating and socializing before bed.

This system does not need daylight savings time because nighttime never changes. Night is night. Due to the seasons, sometimes it breaks closer to what the watch might call 6:00 pm, and at other times it's closer to 7:00 pm or 8:00 pm. That leads to a longer workday over the summer months and much longer nights 6 months later. Overall, this is definitely different from the cultural attitudes reflected by the phrase "9 to 5."

Another example of sociocultural linguistics is the the male-female communication gap. Linguist Deborah Tannen offers some insight into the roots of male-female misunderstanding. She looks at the ways boys and girls play in the US and argues that our socialization during childhood manifests itself in the way we communicate as adults.

Boys in the US, according to Tannen, are raised to value larger group play while girl play groups tend to be smaller and more intimate. And those smaller play groups can produce girls who've learned, better than boys, how to build ties with friends.

Ultimately, Tannen says that males learn to embolden friendship by talking about all the cool stuff

males do together. Women develop a different culture of friendship. Specifically, they are much better attuned to the subterranean messages, or meta-messages, of even the most basic conversations.

Tannen isn't saying that all women are small-group-oriented people, nor is she saying that all men can't express themselves in terms of their emotional and personal lives. She's simply using sociocultural linguistics to consider gendered differences in the way men and women tend to communicate in the US.

Takeaways

Darwin theorized that language, like biological organisms, evolves from simple to dramatically more complex forms. Essentially, he said that human language emerged from animal communication. That would explain, for instance, how bees can give each other directions, or how wolves manage to organize intricately sophisticated group hunting sessions.

However, human language is so complex that we can reasonably distinguish human language as something remarkably special in the animal kingdom. We can point to biological distinctions of *Homo sapiens* as language users. We share a uniquely human mutation of the FOXP2 gene, which has been directly linked to human language formation as well as spatial orientation.

We also have intricately evolved bodies: Consider our mouths, lungs, and brains. We can orchestrate all of these in microseconds to produce just the right sequence of noise to easily communicate any idea that crosses our minds.

Human language did nothing short of change the very nature of evolution itself. With language, humans collectively increased our capacity for information exchange. Information exchange dramatically speeds up the development of new technology—and technology extends our biologically evolved abilities.

Thanks to human language, we can now fly like birds and dive into the depths like whales. We can heat our homes in winter and keep them cool in summer. In short, human language has increased our ability to adapt.

But, of course, this adaptation through language and technology can have a dark side—as the very power we use to create can also be used to destroy. Perhaps by understanding the history, structure, and cultural aspects of communication, we'll collectively find a way to make language work for, rather than against, our continued survival.

Suggested Reading

Berwick and Chomsky, *Why Only Us*.

Burling, *The Talking Ape*.

Fouts and Mills, *Next of Kin*.

Tannen, *That's Not What I Meant!*

Questions to Consider

1. What are primate calls, and how do they provide a window into the evolution of human language?

2. How are anthropologists and others working to preserve endangered languages?

3. How can the language we speak impact the way we perceive the world around us?

Apocalyptic Anthropology

Anthropologists can survey the whole of human history and can examine the various ways that humans have envisioned the end of our species. But more than this, anthropologists can also look for critical lessons from the collapse of some of the greatest civilizations on Earth. Maybe these earlier civilizations can provide us some prescient counsel on how to best sustain our lives, our species, and our planet. That's this lecture's focus—a topic we might call apocalyptic anthropology.

Eschatology

Broadly, the term *eschatology* refers the study of humanity's destiny. Different religions have different takes on eschatology. Despite all the nuances, world religions tend to fall into 1 of 2 categories on this subject.

Some religious traditions like Buddhism and Hinduism have a more circular conceptualization of our destiny, while others like Islam and Christianity tend to be more linear, with a clear beginning and end.

This lecture will take a look at what Buddhists, Hindus, Zoroastrians, and the Hopi have to share when it comes to thinking about the apocalypse.

Eschatology: Buddhism

Many people grow up learning that the Buddha was a man who lived sometime between the 6th and 4th centuries B.C.E. and that his name was Siddhartha Gautama. But it may come as a surprise to learn that this famous Siddhartha was actually the 28th Buddha.

Buddhist traditions describe long, epic cycles in which the teachings of the Buddha eventually disappear from the earth without a trace. According to this teaching, we are in the period of the 1st sun, and eventually, a series of 7 new suns will flare up in the sky, turning our planet into a giant, fiery ball before it explodes into oblivion.

On the plus side, destruction is followed by rebirth—a new cycle of existence. And in each cycle, our lifespans can increase or decrease, depending on the collective conduct of humankind.

Eschatology: Hinduism

Hindu cosmologies include three major deities: Brahma, the creator; Shiva, the destroyer, and Vishnu, the universe's protector, who repeatedly returns to Earth to serve this duty. The incarnation that most non-Hindus may have heard about is Krishna, Vishnu's 8th incarnation.

Even with Vishnu's protection, our universe won't last forever. Brahma creates the universe with a shelf life of about 4.32 billion human years. The bad news is that it appears as if we're in Kali Yuga, the 4th and final phase of our current epic cycle.

Vishnu is expected to make a final visit before this particular universe comes to an end. Vishnu is set to return on a white horse as his 10th incarnation, Kalki. Kalki will raise an army and destroy absolutely everything. But Brahma will set the whole process in motion yet again. And with a new epoch in its infancy, humanity will be restored to a golden age in communion with the gods, and with lifespans of 100,000 years.

This cycle will repeat eternally. Even when Brahma dies after trillions of human years, a new Brahma is born to repeat yet another cycle.

Eschatology: Zoroastrianism

Zoroastrianism dates back to well over 3000 years ago in Iran, and it thrived as the region's religious tradition of choice until the 7th century and the spread of Islam.

Structurally, Zoroastrianism resembles aspects of the Judeo-Christian and Islamic tradition, sporting a single god who created the world. The Zoroastrian tradition describes a final cataclysmic battle in which good triumphs over evil. Then, the last messiah, Saoshyans, resurrects the dead, and restores their earthly bodies for final judgment.

Then, in a dramatic flash, the metals in the mountains and hills melt, flooding the earth and forming a molten river. All humans, living and dead, are then shepherded through this burning river.

The righteous tread through in comfort, while the iniquitous collectively perish as the glowing river carries them to hell, where all wickedness in the universe will be destroyed. Those who pass through the molten river receive delightful eternal lives.

Eschatology: The Hopi

In the late 1940s, Hopi elders in America's southwest learned of the development of the atomic bomb and its mushroom cloud. Upon hearing this news, they made a remarkable decision. After keeping it an internal secret for almost 1000 years, they decided to share the Hopi prophecy with the entire planet.

Brahma

The gist of the prophecy is this: Humankind has lived through 3 different worlds, and our current phase, the 4th world, may be drawing to a rapid close. At the end of the 3 previous worlds, the Great Spirit "purified or punished" humanity for corruption, greed, and turning from his ways.

The Great Spirit charged 3 helpers with the task of partnering up with the Hopi to bring peace on earth. If they fail, then it's all over. But if they succeed, humanity would be saved from the terrible day of purification.

Secular Eschatology

Despite the remarkable diversity we see among the world's religious traditions, an awful lot of them allude to a fiery end to humanity. This flame-ridden finale matches up well with how many scientists foresee the end of our planet.

Most scientists predict that in around 5 billion years, the Sun's core will run out of hydrogen, and it will expand to about 250 times its current size. And when that happens, we can expect the Earth to completely vaporize as the Sun swallows it.

But some scientists see the end of humankind as the rise of the machines. What if the physical sciences and computer sciences fused through an irrevocable new machine-human hybrid?

The technologist Ray Kurzweil foresees just such a convergence, and he describes this transition as the singularity. Kurzweil predicts that in 2029, machines will emerge that exhibit intelligent behavior that is indistinguishable from humans. Then, by 2045, computers will be 1 billion times more powerful than all the human brains on Earth combined.

When it comes to the singularity, there are 2 major camps. First, there are people like the technologist Elon Musk, who see the rise of artificial intelligence as the biggest imminent threat to the survival of our species. The other camp sees an evolutionary opportunity to merge with machines once and for all. Regardless of which camp one

favors, it's clear that our biological and technological evolution are becoming progressively intertwined.

Lessons from the Past

This lecture now turns to some of the world's great civilizations to see if their histories of collapse might offer a few lessons about how to avoid extinction.

First up is the great Mesopotamian city of Ur. Well positioned in the Persian Gulf, this small village emerged as one of the earliest cities born of the new agricultural age. But shifting climate patterns and an overuse of resources and land pushed people to migrate from the region. Ur was abandoned and left for ruins in the 4th century B.C.E.

Not too far from Ur, Egypt came to international prominence and regional dominance around 3100 B.C.E. But this didn't last forever.

The agricultural prowess of Egypt fed an immensely productive civilization with great military might. However, regional rivals developed improved metal technologies, namely the Hittites and their iron. As bronze makers, Egypt rose to

prominence, but without access to materials to embrace the Iron Age, their technological slip helped chip away at one of the most celebrated of ancient civilizations.

Similarly, with a reliance on non-local raw materials like timber, Egypt found it harder and harder to sustain its growth, and then its existence. As Egypt weakened, peripheral satellites of the empire rose, and eventually Egypt fell into the grip of a seemingly endless list of conquerors.

Another case comes from southern Africa, just inland from the Swahili Coast. There lie the ruins of Great Zimbabwe, an amazing kingdom that thrived until the 15th century. The ruins are a World Heritage Site with a stunning rock structure at the center.

Hundreds of years ago, Great Zimbabwe was a crucial hub in an international trade network that spread far beyond Africa's Swahili Coast into parts of India, China, and the Middle East.

But by the year 1500, Great Zimbabwe had dropped out of this trade network. Ceramics found at this remarkable site show fewer and fewer imports were arriving as the civilization faded. Some experts argue that drought and overgrazing of cattle took its eventual toll on the surrounding region, and that made it tougher and tougher to feed the thousands of people who lived in Great Zimbabwe.

Like Ur and Egypt, Great Zimbabwe may have collapsed as a victim of its own success. With a remarkable capacity for growth and food production, these civilizations ran like a runaway train—until they ran out of fuel.

The final stop on this lecture's survival tour brings us to another World Heritage Site, this time in North America. The site is a place we call Cahokia; it's not far from modern-day St. Louis, Missouri.

The climate record shows that the site experienced violent and frequent floods for millennia. Then, as these floods tapered off, people settled what would become the magnificent Cahokia. Humans were quick to dig in and cultivate the rich local soil. Populations grew and flourished, and by the mid-11th century, Cahokia had become the first known megacity in North America.

They created woodhenges positioned to mark solstices. The woodhenges were basically a sylvan version of the stone structures found at Stonehenge in the U.K. But with every house, temple, and woodhenge built with wood, Cahokians depleted the forests that supported the rapid rise of this civilization. And it was this deforestation that altered the Cahokia watershed, bringing back unforgiving floods.

The collapse of Cahokia is certainly a complex phenomenon, but there's no doubt that deforestation and the return of violent floods undermined everything that once made it the largest North American city on record, a title it held all the way until Philadelphia in the mid-1700s.

The Lesson

What does the collapse of past civilizations teach us about our status as the sole surviving hominins? For starters, the archaeological record clearly warns us that we need to be thinking seriously about climate change and our use of fossil fuels. We need to come up with new options and solutions.

Stonehenge

Past civilizations transformed the human experience, yet they all faded away, one way or another. They share the same story arc: Humans find a great place for innovative food production; they parlay their food surplus into a full-fledged, urban civilization; but ultimately, they fail to sustain themselves.

And while climate fluctuations and our natural resource use alone can't take the rap or credit for the rise and fall of civilizations, they certainly play a significant role. It's a role that we'd do well to better understand. After all, for 200,000 years now, humans have displayed an uncanny knack for adapting to a wondrous array of ecologies and environments. It's up to us to extend that record.

Suggested Reading

Bostrom and Cirkovic, *Global Catastrophic Risks*.

Kolbert, *The Sixth Extinction*.

Kurzweil, *The Singularity Is Near*.

Shanahan, *The Technological Singularity*.

Questions to Consider

1. How do world religions and secular technologists envision the end of humankind?

2. As 21st-century humans, what are some of the lessons we can learn from previous world civilizations that flourished for centuries but then crashed into oblivion nonetheless?

3. How might humanity's remarkable fascination with imagining the end of times help us survive, for at least a little bit longer?

Cultural Anthropology and Human Diversity

C ultural anthropology builds bridges of understanding. It connects people across all kinds of linguistic and cultural boundaries. And, the more we understand other ways of seeing and being in the world, the more we actually understand ourselves as individuals and as a species. This lecture visits a few anthropologists across the world to learn how anthropology reconciles the infinite cultural diversity of humankind with the biological fact that we are one race, *Homo sapiens*.

Edward Burnett Tylor

The English anthropologist was the first professional anthropologist to publish a comprehensive definition of culture. We find his definition of culture in his 1871 book *Primitive Culture*. There, Tylor asserts that culture is "that complex whole which includes knowledge, belief, art, morals, law, custom, and any other capabilities and habits acquired by man as a member of society."

His methodology is ethnology. Rather than travel the globe documenting exotic cultures, Tylor and ethnologists explored human cultural diversity by mining libraries and archives. Ultimately, Tylor deployed a comparative approach that blended ethnology, archaeology, and philosophy or reason. One of the central tenets of Tylor's work and of cultural evolutionism is that progress is our dominant narrative.

Edward Burnett Tylor

Lewis Henry Morgan

Another voice behind the primitive/civilized schematic was Lewis Henry Morgan. In the 1840s, the Seneca were engaged in a land dispute with the Ogden Land Company. Morgan helped the Seneca work out a solution to that dispute.

Morgan's fascination with Native American cultures compelled him to break out of the library and into the field. He traveled throughout the US to collect kinship data.

While in the field, Morgan gathered data from government officials known as Indian Agents, and he accumulated missionary data. Curating all these data streams, Morgan noted a distinct kinship pattern he referred to as classificatory kinship.

Essentially, kinship is the way a society organizes social relations in terms of family descent, but Morgan's classificatory kinship includes people who may or may not be genetically related. He noted classificatory kinship patterns across Native Americans and concluded that this form of kinship was a remnant of humanity's primitive state.

Ready to test his idea further, he sought out kinship data from all over the world using a 7-page questionnaire. He compiled his results and found that he could sort kinship patterns into distinct kinship systems that we still teach today. For example, it is common in the US to call one's mother's sister one's aunt, and her children one's cousins. But in some cultures, one would refer to the aunt as mother and her children as siblings, not one's cousins.

In 1877, Morgan published his findings in a major book called *Ancient Society*. The book was fiercely influential on the era's great thinkers and writers like Marx and Engels. In it, Morgan clearly defines cultural evolutionism as a process in 3 phases:

1. The primitive stage, associated with foraging communities.
2. The barbarian stage, brought on by the domestication of plants and animals.
3. The civilized stage, with state-level societies.

Morgan wanted to document earlier-stage cultures because, for him, they were a living window into our less-civilized past. And they were dying out.

Morgan's legacy includes that call for more anthropology, but his true contribution was his vast archive of ethnographic data from all over the world. Additionally, he integrated field research with cultural evolutionism.

However, in the present day, anthropologists are long over the idea that cultural evolution occurs on a progressive spectrum from savage to civilized.

Franz Boas

Why did cultural evolution fall out of favor? The answer takes us to the Arctic, on Baffin Island. In the 1880s, Franz Boas, the father of American anthropology, was there on a 15-month field study.

Unlike Morgan and Tylor, Boas didn't believe in culture grades. Instead, where cultural evolutionists saw savages and barbarians, Boas saw complex, sophisticated people artfully adapted to their unique environment.

Upon arriving on Baffin Island, Boas realized that as long as he was in the Arctic, he was the primitive, and his hosts were the sophisticates. After all, left to his own devices, Boas wouldn't last a night on this frozen island.

Boas saw sophistication in how the Inuit on Baffin Island sustained themselves in such a challenging place to live. What he saw was cultural relativity. Boas didn't do it alone, but he helped change the way we think about culture and each other. His career literally marks anthropology's transition out of cultural evolutionism and into cultural relativity.

How did cultural relativity win out in an era of entrenched cultural evolutionism? Boas did plenty of research and accumulated massive collections of anthropological artifacts. He wrote over 700 books and articles alone.

Perhaps his greatest legacy, however, was the scores of students he mentored. These students went on to build new anthropology programs across the United States, and their names are the giants of early American anthropology:

- Ruth Benedict, who wrote the 1934 public affairs pamphlet *The Races of Mankind*, which articulates cultural relativity from the Boasian perspective.
- Melville J. Herskovits, who set up the anthropology department at Northwestern University.
- Edward Sapir, who created the University of Chicago's famous anthropology program.
- Alfred Kroeber, who created UC Berkeley's famous museum and department of anthropology.

Bronisław Malinowski

Boas had a revolutionary counterpart in England: Bronisław Malinowski. Like Boas, Malinowski was a Physics Ph.D. from continental Europe. He was drawn to anthropology, and he brought his scientific mind and methods to the discipline and his teaching.

He was fervently against the idea of cultural evolution despite the fact that it was the established norm, thanks to the work of people like Tylor. He argued that cultural evolutionism was bad science.

Malinowski did some of his most important work in the Pacific. It was on the Trobriand Islands that Malinowski had his cultural relativity moment, and it's where he invented the concept of functionalism.

Just as Boas saw complex people doing remarkable things to sustain their Arctic lives, Malinowski saw the same rational or functional side to things that others viewed as primitive or exotic. Specifically, he was interested in the logic of local economics.

Here's a brief segment from the book in which Malinowski defines functionalism, *Argonauts of the Western Pacific*. It shows not only Malinowski's beautifully descriptive language, but also his understanding that these so-called natives are anything but primitive:

> A most remarkable form of intertribal trade is that obtaining between the Motu of Port Moresby and the tribes of the Papuan Gulf. The Motu sail for hundreds of miles in heavy, unwieldy canoes, called *lakatoi,* which are provided with characteristic crab-claw sails. They bring pottery and shell ornaments, in olden days, stone blades, to Gulf Papuans, from whom they obtain in exchange sago and the heavy dug-outs, which are used afterwards by the Motu for the construction of their *lakatoi* canoes.

In the early 20th century, this was a new way to understand cultural diversity.

Malinowski instilled the functionalist method in his students. Tylor and the cultural evolutionists had culture, race, and biology all interlinked. But with functionalism, Malinowski separates these concepts. To see the world through functionalist glasses, Malinowski offers us 4 major tenets of the functionalist methodology:

1. Malinowski promoted science-based fieldwork. He said we had to be empiricists. We must follow the scientific model to produce testable and correctable knowledge.

2. Malinowski stressed the importance of cultural immersion as the only way to get a glimpse of daily life and the mindset of people who lead very different lives than anthropologists.

3. Malinowski warned us not to dissect culture traditions down to isolated practices. Instead, he urged students to "study the whole." For example, his Trobriand Islands work focused on understanding the local economic system, but his research included everything about daily life in these communities.

4. Malinowski advised on exactly what kinds of anthropological data to collect while in the field. He mentions 3 data types:

    ›   Type 1 is the institutional outline. Researchers should go in and chart out how the community operates. Who's in charge of what? Who does what? What's the social hierarchy?

    ›   Type 2 is called ethnographic utterances. Malinowski says to record how people actually talk.

    ›   Type 3 is the "imponderabilia of actual life." Put simply, Malinowski wants researchers to write down every single thing they see.

The rich and deep descriptive language in Malinowski's work was made possible by the depths of details in his field notes. In fact, he is a brilliant model for writing about culture. Blending his Western point of view with the perspectives he acquired through cultural immersion, Malinowski invented a new genre of writing: ethnographic realism.

Malinowski also tells us that cultural immersion includes some classic ethnographic tools including doing a census, mapping, language study, surveys, and interviews. Importantly, he recommends a field diary to ensure the separation of objective and subjective data and notes. The subjective (or *etic*) notes are for the diary. The objective (or *emic*) observations are for field notes.

Interviews and census taking are two classic ethnographic tools.

Malinowski and Boas envisioned new ways to decipher cultural diversity in the name of anthropology and science. And the legacies of these early methodologists run deep. They laid bare the 4 cornerstones of modern anthropology:

1. Cultural relativity.
2. Participant observation.
3. The reconciliation of etic and emic perspectives.
4. The critical importance of interdisciplinary research via the 4 subfields of anthropology.

Suggested Reading

Kroeber and Kluckholn, *Culture*.

Stocking, *Observers Observed*.

Tylor, *Primitive Culture*.

Questions to Consider

1. What is cultural evolutionism, and how did early anthropological scholars like E.B. Tylor and Lewis Henry Morgan classify human cultural diversity?

2. What did cultural relativists like Boas and Malinowski do to challenge and eventually discredit cultural evolutionism?

Field Research in Cultural Anthropology

I n the previous lecture, we saw how Franz Boas and Bronislaw Malinowski used their scientific approach to usher in the era of cultural relativity. It was nothing short of revolutionary to move from the dominance of racially charged cultural evolutionism to cultural relativity—but what happened next? This lecture's task is to examine how new generations built on the foundations laid by Boas and Malinowski. We'll also see what new thinkers can teach us about doing ethnographic field research.

Alfred Kroeber

Alfred Kroeber was in his senior year when Franz Boas arrived at Columbia as its 1st professor of anthropology. Kroeber's early intellectual curiosities focused on literature and languages, which is what opened the door to his career as an anthropologist.

One of Boas's popular courses, on Native American languages, attracted Kroeber's attention. This eventually led to an anthropological adventure and 2 years of field research amongst the Arapaho.

He earned his Ph.D. in 1901 on Arapaho symbolism, and Boas's influence is clear. First of all, Kroeber was an empiricist. He embraced the idea that anthropological research should be rooted in the scientific method. Additionally, he carried the torch of cultural relativity and taught by example when it came to cultural immersion.

One of Kroeber's most enduring accomplishments is the creation of the flagship anthropology program at the University of California, Berkeley.

Zora Neale Hurston

One of Boas's notable students was the novelist Zora Neale Hurston. As an African American in the early 20th century, Hurston defied prevailing racial and gender conventions as a student of anthropology at Columbia University.

Boas had a keen interest in researching folklore as a window into cultural diffusion and assimilation. He relished folklore students like Hurston.

Hurston investigated the cultural diffusion aspect of folklore in the Boas tradition, but she did something else: She added an interpretivist approach to the anthropology of folklore.

Hurston not only documented and mapped out the folklore of the American South and the Caribbean. Her new approach produced 2 new and invaluable insights into the anthropological potential of an interpretivist approach to folklore.

Specifically, she noted that once we enter the realm of interpreting and deconstructing folklore, we open a fascinating window into a culture. Moreover, she noted that the otherwise muted voices of female perspectives and voices are rendered visible through folklore.

She also characterized folklore as an adaptive strategy. For instance, the stories of Br'er Rabbit could have been used by slaves raising children in the 18th century. One story involves Br'er Rabbit hiding from a powerful bear in a briar patch.

Such stories always had a trope that served as a thinly veiled lesson on how the powerlessness of slavery could be overcome with cunning and smarts rather than physical force.

Hurston's work provides several methodological lessons:

1. Hurston was masterful at recording not only the thoughts and worldviews of people, but she captured the sounds and rhythms of their speech. This is shown in books like *Their Eyes Were Watching God*, which transport the reader deep into Hurston's worlds.
2. Hurston was relentless in working out ways to gain the trust and partnership of her research communities.
3. Creative approaches to data collection are fun for both anthropologists and informants. For example, while collecting folktales and oral traditions in Florida, Hurston organized a "Big Lies" contest. This got the locals to open up with fantastic tales, one example being about people who were so small they could walk between raindrops during a storm.

Audrey Richards

Audrey Richards was one of Malinowski's star graduates. Richards spent her early years in India during her father's time in the British Colonial Service in Calcutta. She grew up to be an admired field researcher and a tireless and inspiring anthropology professor.

Where Malinowski taught, before going to the field, students were required to write a thesis based on existing literature. Richards embraced the 4-field approach and picked a topic that was as biological as it was cultural: nutrition.

She studied in Zambia with a group that practiced matrilineal descent and kinship. In her words, Richards set out to "make an intensive study of the social institutions, customs and beliefs of the [Bemba] tribe ... with special reference to the part played by women in tribal and economic life... the nature and importance of the family system and the marriage contract... and problems connected with the rearing and education of children."

Richards was essentially planting a seed that eventually grew into a specialization called medical anthropology.

Richards in Zambia

Richards took to field research and loved the anthropology life in Zambia. She rode around on her bicycle, living in Bemba communities and helping women with daily tasks. She also sat and talked with community elders.

Before arriving in the communities, she'd spent a month studying the local language at a remote mission. She was a skilled hunter, and her colleagues and friends described her with words like "fearless" and "inspiring."

Malinowski's empiricism was omnipresent in Richards's original and revolutionary approach. She recorded what individuals ate and weighed food to calculate its nutritional value. Additionally, she calculated the nutritional value of wild and gathered foods.

Her first field study was followed by another in 1933, and in 1939 she published her work in the book *Land, Labour and Diet in Northern Rhodesia*. In the book, she describes the agricultural system of her hosts. She also analyzes the gendered division of labor as well as land use.

Two takeaway ideas stand out:

1. She demonstrated that anthropologists need to seek out indigenous knowledge.
2. In the behavior of their research communities, anthropologists observe complex, local, ecological management systems.

Richards's Legacy

Richards's legacy is multidimensional. She helped preserve and embolden the empiricism and cultural relativity of Malinowski's functionalism. In fact, she wrote a comprehensive history of functionalism, teaching students the practical value of anthropology for colonial policymakers and anyone who studies development and social change.

Additionally, she demonstrated the primacy of fieldwork and the scientific method as principles of anthropological research. Her work opened a new field of medical (or nutritional) anthropology. She also championed bringing women into anthropology and then into the field.

With her focus on the nexus of food, nutrition, and health, Richards was ahead of her time. She promoted practical applications for anthropology, which translated into baby-weighing nutritional studies across Africa and the world.

Richards would be pleased at the vibrancy and growth of the Society for Applied Anthropology. Years before that society was born, Richards advocated a national, applied anthropology program in Britain that could teach basic anthropological theories and methods to government officials and other nontraditional anthropology students.

While rooted in nutritional science, Richards made anthropology stronger by embracing and emboldening the interdisciplinarity of the field.

Edwin Evans-Pritchard

This lecture will close with a visit to one more star in the Malinowski line. His name was Sir Edwin Evans-Pritchard. Evans-Pritchard was born in the UK a year after Kroeber started his position at the University of California, Berkeley. He studied under Malinowski, and he too found new ways to deploy his teacher's methods.

Evans-Pritchard promoted the humanities side of anthropology. Evans-Pritchard collected field data and used his observations to interpret local histories and social structures. His more interpretive approach, and his fascination with social structure, emerged as a new brand of functionalism, now known as structural functionalism.

He refined this approach in the field while studying groups living in East Africa. In his early study in the Sudan, he considered how beliefs and practices in witchcraft among

the Azande people reinforce social cohesion.

In his 1937 book on the subject, he argued that Azande witchcraft functionally operates as a safety valve that redirects conflict and tension. It stabilizes society for the good of the order.

Another one of his major studies emerged in his 1940 book, *The Nuer*, about a group of pastoralists who live in East Africa. Amongst the Nuer, he continued his inquiry into social structure. He wanted to see if his ideas would hold up in a community of pastoralists the way they did among the Azande farmers. He asked: How do less stratified societies work? What does their political organization look like?

Evans-Pritchard saw that cattle, not cash, made Nuer societies work, so he followed the cattle. He learned to relate the chief values and social structure of the Nuer by understanding their relationship and practices with cattle. He characterized the social idiom of the Nuer as a bovine idiom.

Evans-Pritchard creatively diverged from the more empirical work of others like Malinowski and Richards. His great ethnographic details render his books instructive for anyone who wants to write or read about studying culture and social structures.

Suggested Reading

Hurston, *Mules and Men*.

Malinowski, *Argonauts of the Western Pacific*.

Richards, *Land, Labour, and Diet in Northern Rhodesia*.

Questions to Consider

1. As highly influential figures in the history of anthropology, what did Zora Neale Hurston and Edwin Evans-Pritchard build upon the ideas and methods of their teachers?

2. How did Audrey Richard's field research methods presage the emergence of medical anthropology?

Kinship, Family, and Marriage

There is no universal rule about the way humans make families: Humans approach families in all sorts of ways. Anthropology brings a bird's-eye view to make sense of this diversity. This lecture examines a Malian village, some Tibetan farmers, and some people from Amazonia, because we need to investigate why different cultures create families in so many different ways. Throughout, we'll see compelling cross-cultural examples of how different cultures have different ideas about how to structure a family.

Different Family Types

The nuclear family is the kind of family Americans see all over television, from *The Dick Van Dyke Show* to *Family Guy*. In its simplest form, a nuclear family consists of 2 parents and their children. But if we set the nuclear family as the standard definition for family, such ethnocentrism will surely lead to our disappointment.

Generally speaking, in the US, when people start a new family, they tend to start a new household in a new location, separate from their parents. This is referred to as neolocal residence.

For subsistence-farming societies, on the other hand, unilocal residence tends to be the prevailing norm. In one farming community in Mali, for example, males marry females in surrounding villages.

The wedding festivities begin when the bride-to-be, her family, her community, and a host of drummers literally walk to her new home. Grown males may have wives and children of their own, but they live in the same compound they've always lived in. This is unilocal residence.

Family Research

Lewis Henry Morgan did anthropological research on family and kinship before anthropology was taught in American universities. With inspiration from work like Morgan's, early anthropologists were trained to collect kinship data, and to theorize on kinship to understand the social structure of traditional societies.

By the 1940s, kinship was all the rage among anthropologists. For example, Edward Evans-Pritchard wrote *The Nuer* based on his fieldwork with an East African pastoralist group.

He studied the social structure and quotidian life of these cattle-oriented people, and he made the general argument that kinship, or the way we do family, is basically a dynamic rulebook for social relations, albeit an unwritten rulebook. It connects us with each other, defining our relationships with the folks we call family as well as the rest of the world.

From the interpretivist point of view, anthropologist Claude Lévi-Strauss was interested in family and kinship in terms of

marital-based alliances rather than bloodlines or direct descent.

We can put this alliance lens to work in the Malian community of Dissan. While men remain in their birth communities, upon marriage, women in Dissan leave their birth village to live with their husbands. This pattern of marriages weaves a thick matrix of long-established family relationships that transform individual communities into a self-reinforcing and symbiotic cooperative.

Virtual Visit: Tibet

Next, this lecture will take a virtual anthropologic visit to Tibet, where we'll visit the Limi. The Limi are family subsistence farmers who have cultivated this challenging, rocky land for generations. This society practices fraternal polyandry, which is multiple brothers marrying one wife.

As we get into the participant observation spirit, we work

alongside our hosts preparing the fields for the coming rains. Our hosts tell us how difficult it is to grow food here. They have only limited lands that can produce food—and only then through grueling manual labor.

As we sit in the glow of a solar lantern writing our field observations, we need to write down everything we observed and learned today. But how does this information address the primary research question: Why is it that brothers share a wife?

When asked, our hosts kept saying that fraternal polyandry is just how people do things around here. Furthermore, if every brother had a wife, there would be way too many kids and not enough food.

They love kids but they fear having too many. Plus, they have to deal with food insecurity, manual farming, limited land, limited inputs and resources, and no real other work to be had in this remote region. The more we look at this fraternal polyandry from a Limi perspective, the more it begins to make sense.

Ultimately, with the help of our host community, we not only got a glimpse into their lives, values, and strong work ethic, but we also figure out why fraternal polyandry is the most rational and appropriate local strategy for sustaining life and building a family with new generations to come.

Fraternal polyandry would keep birthrates lower because not everyone has kids concurrently. Secondly, it prevents the breakup of family farms. In Limi, when the household head passes away, the household holdings stay together as a cooperative unit. In the US, by contrast, siblings might split up inheritance and property and then continue on distinct paths.

Virtual Visit: Venezuela

Our next visit takes us to Venezuela to visit the Bari people. They live in Amazonia. Here, our mission is to answer the question: How can it be that some children in the Amazon reportedly have multiple biological fathers?

The anthropologist Stephen Beckerman has spent decades visiting and studying the Bari. He explains that we're visiting with an indigenous group who fish, hunt, and grow manioc and bananas. Thanks to Beckerman's presence, a few elders are willing to talk about their fatherhood beliefs.

The Bari elders explain that for a Bari child to be born, a single insemination was not ample enough, and that healthy newborns required what they call multiple sperm washes. Biological parents will likely continue to fertilize their pre-born baby, and it's common that a second male will provide secondary so-called washes.

The idea of multiple biological fathers clearly violates everything we've been taught about how babies are born. But with our anthropological lens and mission, we can see some terrific reasons for this cultural idea and practice.

Beckerman explains that the Bari have long suffered from attacks and raids that sometimes decimate entire communities. The Bari themselves are a peaceful group, but, since the arrival of the conquistadors in the 16th century, generations of Bari people have been stricken with massacres and other attacks from outsiders.

In the 1940s and 1950s for example, regional cattle ranchers regularly massacred Bari villages in a campaign to claim their land. And in the 21st century, it is oil and coal companies who are maneuvering to seize Bari lands.

The point is that they've adapted to a life of recurring attacks and stress. Beckerman interviewed 897 Bari women who reported on over 900 pregnancies. Women have an average of 8 pregnancies, but stillbirth and infant mortality rates were quite high.

Unlike all other arrangements, women who bring in a secondary father actually had lower incidents of stillbirths and miscarriages. Having a secondary father is, at least here among the Bari, a proven way to increase the likelihood that a child will survive into puberty.

The Bari are not alone. There are indigenous groups with similar practices and beliefs across South America, India, and Papua New Guinea.

Ecological resources and geography can shape how we create families.

Though their understanding of human biology may be off, they still get the important question right. They know what to do to increase their children's chances of reaching adulthood.

Diversity of Ideas

People across the world think about and practice kinship in all kinds of different ways. The diversity of kinship approaches tells us there isn't a gold standard for how to do marriage or family.

In fact, we've discovered the exact opposite. Our ecological resources and geography really can shape the way we successfully create and sustain our families. And there isn't one single form of family that works for all socioeconomic and cultural contexts.

Suggested Reading

Evans-Pritchard, *The Nuer.*

Hrdy, *Mothers and Others.*

Lévi-Strauss, *The Elementary Structures of Kinship.*

Questions to Consider

1. What is kinship, and why do anthropologists dedicate so much attention to studying kinship, marriage, and family across cultures?

2. How do environmental and economic conditions help explain the presence of fraternal polyandry among the Limi of Tibet, as well as the phenomenon of partible paternity in the Venezuelan Amazon?

Sex, Gender, and Sexuality

T he past several lectures have examined human diversity and cultural traditions. Today's anthropologists continue to test and correct their understanding of human diversity. Anthropologists started with cultural evolutionism, but now understand biology and culture as distinct facets of humanity. This lecture takes a similar approach with sex and gender. It uses anthropology to see how biological sex, gender, and sexuality are unique threads of humanity.

Intersex Individuals

A hermaphrodite is an organism that has both male and female sex organs. Hermaphrodites comprise a relatively small category within a larger group of people who, biologically, have both male and female sexual traits.

The term *intersex* is used to describe this group, whose biology is not exclusively female and male. This is strictly in reference to physiology—not sexual orientation.

Some people are born intersex. According to Anne Fausto-Sterling, the rate is 1.7%, which is a higher incidence than albinism.

In the US, cultural and medical practices have classified intersex as a deformity rather than diversity. As such, it's often the case that when intersex children are born, doctors and parents typically go into emergency mode. They make a decision: male or female. Shockingly, the decision to go male or female is commonly made immediately, based on the presence or absence of a functional penis. Many parents will opt for their child to have a so-called corrective surgery.

Studies have shown that people who received this sexual assignment surgery are at risk for gender identity issues later in life. Operating on the body can clear up biological ambiguity when it comes to sex organs, but those organs do not control one's sexuality or gender identity. Rather than reinforcing a non-biological duality of male and female, perhaps we should expand our understanding of other sexes.

Intersex Categories

Under the general term intersex, there are various categories based on different biological characteristics. The biologist Joan Roughgarden wrote the book *Evolution's Rainbow*, in which we can see that intersex and non-binary sexes are more than common throughout the entire animal kingdom. Roughgarden discusses several types of intersexuality.

First, there are hermaphrodites. Despite the fact that this may be the most recognized or familiar form of intersex, it's actually the rarest of them all. The ratio is 1 in 85,000. A hermpaphrodite usually has some combination of testes, ovaries, or ovotestis, which contain both ovarian and testicular tissue.

Hypospadias are more common. Hypospadia is considered to be minor if the vent is off-center on the tip of the penis. To one degree or another, this occurs in over 40% of males. But then, around 1 in 2000 males are born hypospadias major, which means that the vent is anywhere but the tip of the penis.

Even more common than hypospadias is chromosomal variation. This outcome happens about once in 1000 births. These varieties of intersex occur as the result of an additional chromosome. Instead of an XX female or an XY chromosome male, the combinations XXY, XYY, XXX, or even XXYY might occur.

The takeaway from this discussion: Biological sex isn't really a binary male-female concept.

Sexuality and Gender

Sexuality and gender are not strictly biological phenomena. That's why cultural anthropology can help us see the distinct qualities of biological sex as opposed to one's sexuality and gender.

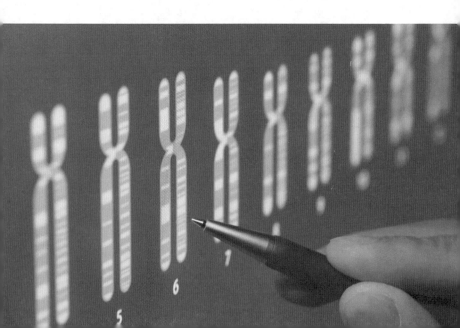

Darwin and his contemporaries may have argued that we're ultimately all one race, *Homo sapiens*. But they were clear that half the human race wasn't built for thinking or anything else outside of the domestic sphere. They believed that women's role in human reproduction is so physically and mentally demanding that it limits their potential as scholars, doctors, and presidents.

A brilliant French scientist named Clémence Royer challenged this idea. She was hired but then fired by Darwin as the translator of his masterpiece, *On the Origins of Species*. When she had a disagreement with Darwin, she let it be known. After her firing, she continued her scientific career.

She gave a remarkable and courageous speech to the Société d'Anthropologie de Paris in 1874. She was ahead of her times and most of anthropology with her succinct take on gender. Here's what she said:

> Up until now, science like law, made exclusively by men, has too often considered woman as an absolutely passive being, without instincts or passions or her own interests; as a purely plastic material capable of taking any form given her without resistance; a being without the inner resources to react against the education she receives or against the discipline to which she submits as part of law, custom or opinion. Woman is not made like this.

Royer's critique of European science in the late 19th century opened the door to a more comprehensive study of humanity—an anthropology that saw women in their fullness as human beings.

The Zuni

Undeniably, Western gender traditions strongly separate men's roles from women's roles, thus developing a gender binary that is closely tied to the biology binary. But cultural anthropologists have found and documented world cultures that don't have a strict male-female gender binary.

One example comes from the Zuni of the American Southwest, where scholars like Will Roscoe have studied Native American cultures and the presence of two-spirit people. Practices and norms certainly differed between distinct Native American groups, but the presence of two-spirit people was rather common.

Two-spirit people are sometimes referred to as a 3rd or 4th gender. They clearly contradict the male-female gender binary. Typically, the two-spirited person is celebrated as a gifted member of society who may perform trades or skills that are associated with the so-called opposite sex.

According to the literature, two-spirit people were not necessarily homosexual, but some were. They were not dressing or acting with the intent to deceive fellow community members; rather, they were known and admired publicly for possessing both male and female qualities.

For example, among the Zuni, when a potential two-spirit child emerges, a ritual served as a test to discern who this person truly was, regardless of biology. In one version, a bow and arrow is placed next to a basket, and the young child is asked to pick the one they like the most. If a young girl picks up the bow and arrow, she is celebrated and accepted as a two-spirited person, and she will likely go

on with life learning skills traditionally taught to biological males.

Native Americans aren't the only ones who see more than 2 genders. India has the hijras, and in the Balkans are people called the sworn virgins. In the Pacific are the fakaleitis of Tonga and the mahu of Hawaii. And there are others. What all these cultures and people have in common is a separation of biological sex, gender, and sexuality.

Sexuality

If gender isn't sexuality, and if biological sex doesn't determine sexuality, then what exactly is sexuality? Neuroanthropologists tell us that sexuality does in fact have biological foundations. Multiple studies confirm statistically significant correlations between human sexuality and several biological indicators, including the nerve cells in the hypothalamus.

The hypothalamus is located at the center of the brain and produces hormones. Inside the hypothalamus are suprachiasmatic nuclei (or SCN). The SCN, which controls our circadian body rhythm, is closer to some of the biological roots of our sexuality.

Research by noted neurobiologist Dick Swaab and others reveals a relationship between SCN size and homosexuality. Simply put, the SCNs of homosexual men are larger than the SCNs in heterosexual men. They're about twice as large in terms of physical size and the total amount of neurons.

If the SCN of homosexual men are around twice the size of their heterosexual counterparts, how will the SCNs in homosexual men compare with heterosexual females? As it turns out, female SCNs are much smaller than even heterosexual males, meaning women have smaller SCNs and therefore fewer SCN neurons.

Swaab and others like the neurobiologist Simon LeVay also identified another compelling connection between our brains and our sexuality. They identified a nucleus that is understood as the sexually dimorphic nucleus. It's called INAH-3, which is short for the 3rd interstitial nucleus of the anterior hypothalamus.

Like the SCN, the INAH-3 is significantly larger in males than females, and even larger in heterosexual males than in homosexual males and heterosexual females. Overall, the INAH-3 is smaller in people who are sexually attracted to males.

One last connection comes from the hypothalamus, which helps us with our olfactory system. Scientists looked into how the hypothalamus responds to the smells of estrogen (as found in female urine) and testosterone (from male sweat). The results were definitive.

The hypothalamus of people who were sexually attracted to women (heterosexual men and homosexual women) responded to the estrogen. The hypothalamus of people attracted to men, including both homosexual men and heterosexual women, responded to testosterone.

Twin Studies

Roughgarden's exploration of sexuality and biological sex, *Evolution's Rainbow*, provides a great bird's-eye view of twin studies that have looked at sexuality. Collectively, these studies ask the question: Is there evidence for the biological foundations of sexuality?

The studies compare identical versus fraternal twins. The thought is that if homosexuality is in fact biologically based, identical twins who are both gay would be more common than fraternal twins who are both gay.

When researchers tested this theory, they found it was accurate. A 2015 University of California study presented at the American Society of Human Genetics examined the genomes of 47 sets of identical twins. Thirty-seven of the sets had 1 homosexual twin and 1 heterosexual twin. The remaining 10 sets, just over 20% of the study population, all identified as homosexuals.

Those results are quite revealing. For instance, the fact that over 20% of the twin sets had 2 gay twins indicates that there is something biological going on here.

However, not all identical twins mirror each other's sexuality. In twin sets with at least 1 gay twin, a large number had heterosexual counterparts. Therefore, biology is at work, but there's more to it.

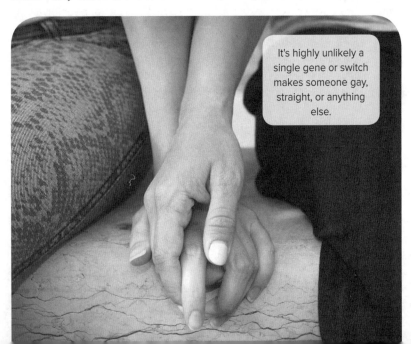

It's highly unlikely a single gene or switch makes someone gay, straight, or anything else.

The most fascinating ideas from this research relate to epigenetics. We have much more to learn before we'll truly understand our epigenetics. But this study of homosexual twins sees that our sexuality may also be influenced by sets of chemical markers that lie between, not within our genes.

The epigenome basically turns our genes on and off in response to a particular moment. Unlike our actual genome, the epigenome is constantly changing. Researchers explored the twin pairs' epigenomes, searching for patterns that could be predictive for sexuality.

In 9 different regions of the epigenome, that's exactly what they found. Their approach appears to be able to biologically identify homosexuality with a 70% accuracy rate.

That study and the hypothalamus studies all point to a common consensus: There are biological foundations of human sexuality. It's important to note that based on today's existing research, it's highly unlikely that there's a single gene or switch that makes someone gay, straight, or anything else. There's something much more complex going on, and we still have much to learn.

Suggested Reading

Harvey, *Almost a Man of Genius*.

Nelson, *Women in Antiquity*.

Peletz, *Gender Pluralism*.

Roughgarden, *Evolution's Rainbow*.

Questions to Consider

1. What specifically is the difference between biological sex, gender, and sexuality?

2. How do mainstream 21st-century ideas on gender and gender identity compare with the way people understood these concepts in Darwin's day?

3. Why are some people born neither fully male nor female?

Religion and Spirituality

Anthropology is the study of humankind. If we want to understand humanity, there are few topics more important than religion. After all, religion is one of the ways we make sense of our lives, our universe, and even our morality. And while it is true humans have used religious differences to exact horrific violence and emotional pain upon each other, religion is also the source of unfathomable love and belonging in the form of selflessness and communion. This lecture takes an anthropological look at religion. The lecture traces its origins and examines how anthropologists have changed some of their thinking on religion.

Animal Grief

Ritual burials, feasts, cave art, and even primatology provide a fairly comprehensive glance at the origins and development of the human religious experience.

Modern apes, including nonhuman apes, express empathy and mourn the loss of others. Biological anthropologists like Barbara King argue that the empathy and mourning we observe in nonhuman apes gives us insight into the roots of the human religious experience.

One example is a famous gorilla named Koko. Koko is a special gorilla who is uniquely suited to bond with her human caretakers, as she has mastered American Sign Language. She showed grief when her companion gorilla passed in the year 2000. She had a similar reaction when she learned of the death of the comedian Robin Williams, with whom she had a bond.

The compassion, empathy, and mourning we see in apes like Koko give us great clues about the foundation, or early roots, of the human religious experience. Empathy and mourning are not religion in themselves. But over generations and generations, they can evolve into what we recognize as modern world religions.

Parietal Art

Parietal art is early art found on cave walls or rocks. Dating back tens of thousands of years, the world's parietal art collectively documents our pre-modern religious life.

One example is a mysterious supernatural image of a therianthrope found in southern France at a site named Trois-Frères. Dating back to around 13,000 B.C.E., the therianthrope is half man, half animal. His finely detailed figure with muscular legs and antlers dominates the large cavern, known as the sanctuary, that houses it. It was likely used for shamanistic rituals and trances.

Archaeologists call this image the sorcerer. It's one of our earliest images of the pre-modern religious experience.

Parietal art is a great window into pre-modern religious life, and it shows that early *Homo sapiens* practiced shamanism. They contemplated alternative universes and what happens after death.

Burials

Archaeological evidence supports the theory that humans, and even Neanderthals, were thinking of the great beyond and doing purposeful burials as early as 90,000 years ago.

In Israel's Qafzeh cave, archaeologists found bones and fragments from over 24 burials. Nearby, on Mount Carmel, archaeologists discovered purposeful burials dating over 100,000 years ago.

The most famous Neanderthal burial is called the Old Man, and he was found purposely buried by others. Because he was old, frail, and essentially toothless, his remains show us that he had a small community who must have cared for him in his old age and upon death.

Modern World Religions

Around 3000 B.C.E., we begin to see archaic religious traditions and rituals emerging in Mesopotamia, then Egypt, China, and eventually in Greek, Celtic, and Native American cultures.

Determining start dates for religions can be tricky. Some religions, like Judaism, can be considered to have a more specific date such as the year 1812 B.C.E. That was when Abraham made his covenant with God.

But other religions, like Hinduism, have a more nebulous starting point unless we pick an important date like the creation of the Upanishads text around 700 B.C.E.

Around 2500 years ago, humankind began to develop one religion after another. Jainism emerged around 600 B.C.E., with Zoroastrianism not long after that. Buddhism arrived right around 400 B.C.E.

Christianity emerged around the year 30 C.E. Islam came around 600 years later. More recently, Sikhism began in the 1400s, followed by the Baha'i and Mormon faiths in the 1800s. In the 20th century, we developed new religious traditions including Rastafarianism and the Jehovah's Witnesses.

By the time Edward Burnett Tylor and anthropology emerged in the late 1800s, the work of 2 scholars forged the foundation for what later becomes the anthropology of religion.

Émile Durkheim

The anthropology of religion essentially starts with the sociologist Émile Durkheim. In one of his most important works, *The Elementary Forms of The Religious Life*, Durkheim explains religion as a social phenomenon that hinders our selfish, individualistic proclivities, and instead promotes social cooperation.

For Durkheim, religious symbols used during religious rituals help reinforce this collective consciousness and cooperation. And as a result, individuals are dependent on society, as they are on God.

Durkheim points out that societies classify all things into 2 piles: the sacred or the profane. The sacred is the social, the ideal, and the divine; the profane is the personal, physical, and earthly realms. Ultimately, in any religion, rituals help promote and prescribe that which is sacred, and thus allow us

Buddhism arrived right around 400 B.C.E.

the opportunity to dwell within the sacred ourselves.

James Frazer

In 1890, James Frazer published another foundational text on the anthropology of religion: *The Golden Bough*. This immensely popular book was a compendium of accounts of world religious practices and knowledge.

Frazer's big idea was that archaic religions were basically fertility cults, and they provided opportunities to worship and make periodic offerings or sacrifices to a sacred king.

He also concluded that the great arc of the human religious experience takes humanity from an initial magical phase, through to religious belief, and then culminating in scientific thought.

Origins of Evolutionism

Frazer, like Tylor and many of his contemporaries, were cultural evolutionists who were keen on studying so-called primitive religions. That's because they were searching for clues about the origins of religion as a sociocultural phenomenon.

In their search for those origins, they went with cultural evolution or social Darwinism. To cultural evolutionists, the monotheism of the Abrahamic faiths was the most advanced form of religious belief. Other religions lagged behind at a lingering evolutionary pace.

According to these folks, advanced religions focus on texts, while primitive religions are oral traditions. In addition, advanced religions focus on the afterlife and are universal in scope. They apply across cultures, unlike primitive religions, which are more culturally specific.

Finally, advanced religions compartmentalize the sacred and profane, but in primitive religions, religion and daily life are organically intertwined and inseparable.

Tylor was in line with that school of thought on the evolution of religion. The racial context of cultural evolutionism tarnishes Tylor's legacy as one of the earliest anthropologists, but he is still widely regarded as a pioneer in the anthropology of religion.

Tylor assumed that the stages of humanity's material "advancement" also corresponded with parallel stages of our spiritual nature. Oddly, Tylor himself had interests outside the confines of conventional monotheism. He didn't write about this publicly, but he was into the Spiritualist movement, intrigued by claims of their evidence that the human personality continues after death.

Functionalism and Cultural Relativity

Tylor and cultural evolutionists weren't the only people investigating world religions. Some rising anthropology stars, like Franz Boas and Bronisław Malinowski, emerged around the turn of the 20th century. They refused to accept the pseudoscience of social Darwinism and the cultural evolutionists.

These men and their scores of students were a new and highly influential wave of cultural relativists. And they were curious about sociocultural functions of religion, very much in the Durkheim tradition.

In a 1925 essay on religion, Malinowski distinguishes the difference between magic and religion. Drawing on Frazer's magic-religion-science discussion, he says that magic is always utilitarian, and magic rituals are generally expected to get specific results, like healing a sick stomach.

Religion was different. Specifically, religious rituals usually focus on more ambiguous results. People don't take communion or fast for a month because they expect a priest cure their ills.

Malinowski and the cultural relativists did long-term participant-observation field research. Living day-to-day with their research communities, the cultural relativists ended up paying much less attention to the origins of religion. Instead, they sought to unveil the inner mindset of the people, including the practical and rational nature of their religious life and rituals. For them, the anthropology of religion was about deciphering the sociocultural function of rituals and religious life.

Cultural relativity in the anthropology of religion endured well into the 20th century, with students of Malinowski and Boas taking their questions to new regions and new people.

One Malinowski student who worked in Africa among pastoralists and farmers, Edward Evans-

Pritchard, focused on social systems. He looked into local religious practices of his East African study communities.

When he did, he broke away from the primitive/modern lens. Instead, he portrayed the rational and functional dimensions of religious practice. His main argument was that for the Azande and Nuer people, as well as any other group, rituals sustain and moderate social structures.

Interpretivist and Feminist Approaches

An emerging interpretivist critique of strict empiricist anthropology stemmed from the idea that regardless of how long an anthropologist does field research, he or she will never get a full and truly authentic picture.

These critiques ushered in yet another way for anthropologists to explore and understand religion. The new phase often focused inward rather than outward, and its holy grail was the search for meaning: symbolism and interpreting myths.

Two preeminent figures, Claude Levi-Strauss and Clifford Geertz, took this less empirical approach to understanding world religions and the religious experience in general.

Levi-Strauss explored the idea that universally, humans are wired to see and understand our world through binaries like raw versus cooked, wild verus civilized, and sacred versus profane. Religion, he wrote, works to mediate these binaries.

Clifford Geertz's anthropological definition of religion summarizes the way many anthropologists approach religion in their work today. Simply put, Geertz says that religion is how we make meaning. To paraphrase: Religion is a system of symbols, which motivate and emotionally resonate with people. It does this by articulating a general order of existence that gives meaning to our lives.

Beyond Levi-Strauss and Geertz, scholars continued to look at the structural and symbolic dimensions of religion. Researchers have developed even more ways to anthropologically cast even more light on humanity's diverse religious practices or beliefs, despite the structural unity of the human religion experience.

One example: Some feminist approaches look at religion as a social institution with gendered relations of power. Feminists have also enriched the anthropology of religion by examining female deities and goddess cultures in pre-Judeo-Christian times.

Suggested Reading

Frazer, *The Golden Bough*.

King, *Evolving God*.

Lowie, *Primitive Religion*.

Questions to Consider

1. What are some of the roots of the human religious experience, and when did it emerge in the evolution of our species?

2. How did Boas and Malinowski explain the existence of religion, and how did their ideas differ from what earlier theorists like E.B. Tylor and Morgan first said?

Art and Visual Anthropology

Whether we're aware of it or not, our cultural background impacts the way we see and understand the world. And nowhere is this fact more clearly on display than when we compare the visual arts of various cultures around the globe. This lecture does some of that comparative work. We'll start by asking: What is art? Then, we'll see how, in the 20th century, new perspectives emerged to challenge outmoded assessments of non-Western art. Next, we'll move to the work of visual anthropology and the history of ethnographic films to see how video technologies can both support and complicate anthropological missions.

What Is Art?

There is no clear line distinguishing art from non-art. For some, art is about technical prowess, while for others, it's about imagination. And then there are others still, who might focus on message or level of abstraction.

The question of what art is has only grown thornier as anthropologists have expanded our cultural horizons. Over the 20th century, Western anthropologists and art historians grappled with the way they should categorize non-Western art.

When anthropologists and others first examined the art of the ancient Aztecs or the art of Africa more generally, they labeled it "primitive" art. But is this is a helpful way to look at non-Western art? Consider the *ciwara* sculpture that is a unifying symbol among the Bamana people of West Africa.

The *ciwara* depicts an antelope, which is carved out of wood and features intricate details in the horns, face, body, and mane. Some brilliant *ciwara* pieces were made recently by sculptors who live in Bamako, the capital city of

Mali. These artists are modern, not primitive, and so are their sculptures.

But there was a time when anthropology identified African art and the *ciwara* as primitive art, whether it was produced 500 years or 1 day ago. Early anthropologists like Edward Burnett Tylor viewed Africans as primitive humans, so that's how they categorized African art and cultures.

The Mid-20th Century and Art in Anthropology

Things changed around the middle of the 20th century, when new generations of anthropologists staked new territory on the interpretivist or symbolic side of the discipline. Rather than testing and correcting theories built on materialist, empirical data, these anthropologists embraced the immeasurable interpretive dimensions of the human experience.

With an eye for interpretation, symbolic anthropologists like Claude Levi-Strauss and Victor Turner embraced artistic expressions as treasure troves of cultural insight and data. In his classic book, *The Savage Mind*, Levi-Strauss described artists as hybrids that are part scientist and part craftsman—or what he calls a bricoleur. The craftsman builds a material object, but that object is an object of knowledge. It contains an entire worldview.

In an ever more connected world, people in the mid-20th century were more exposed to non-Western art and cultures than those who lived just a few decades before. And this art captured the imagination of the West. People considered an African mask a look into Africa and Africans themselves.

Pablo Picasso developed his cubist perspective in large part through his appreciation and emulation of African masks and sculpture. African masks plainly have ears, eyes, and a mouth. They clearly represent a person, or perhaps an antelope. But they aren't like any real-life person or antelope; for instance, they might have elongated noses or sharp points for ears.

Viewed from the side, or in different light, these masks transform. It's almost like the carver

African masks

created the mask using more than 1 set of eyes. That's essentially the inspiration for Picasso's cubism: All those strange shapes and forms are multiple perspectives, visualized at once.

The Late 20th Century

The extinction of the term *primitive art* occurred as anthropologists continued to expand the ways they looked at art. New research themes emerged to look at the sociocultural context of art, the politics of representation, and even the repatriation of art to places like Mali, Egypt, and Greece.

The sociologist Howard Becker was a leading figure in the movement to understand art as a sociocultural process, not just as objects produced by artists. In one of his most celebrated texts, *Art Worlds*, he reframes art as a cooperative network of everyone who participates in the production of art. There's the artist of course, but there are also the people who make and sell art supplies, dealers, critics, consumers, installation experts, business managers, and so on.

Recording an event may change the behavior of the people taking part in the event.

With social Darwinism subsumed by cultural relativity, anthropologists found it no longer tenable to classify non-Western art as primitive. The *ciwara* sculpture isn't more primitive than the Mona Lisa; it's just from a different art world.

Visual Anthropology

Visual anthropology is an inclusive specialization that examines humanity by studying performance, media, and media technologies. Perhaps the most well-known aspect of visual anthropology is ethnographic photography and film—doing anthropology with cameras.

Since the early days of anthropology, researchers have used still and moving images to document and analyze culture. And the evolution of ethnographic film, aided by remarkable developments in sound and camera technology, inspired anthropologists to incorporate progressively more and more of the emic perspectives of their research populations.

Film captures body language and the environment surrounding whatever is being filmed—whether that's a ritual, a performance, or any other aspect of daily life. These are details we don't get from interviews, surveys, and other anthropological methods.

One caveat: The presence of a camera can change a person's behavior. For example, someone might put more effort into their appearance if they know a camera is going to be around. This is called cinestance.

Nanook of the North

Nanook of North, from 1922, was the first major anthropology film, and it helped pioneer the documentary film genre. The filmmaker, Robert Flaherty, filmed episodes from the daily lives of Arctic people, and audiences loved this rare and close-up glance into Inuit life.

Modern critics, however, have critiqued Flaherty for leaving out all signs of modernity. Despite the presence of his equipment, not to mention modern conveniences at the local trading post, Flaherty chose to show only scenes that portrayed an illusion of the pristine and so-called primitive state of Inuit people living off the frigid land.

This was before the era of documentary film, so it's not surprising that Flaherty violated a few of the cardinal rules that would later define the genre. For example, the scenes and people he shares with the audience aren't entirely authentic. He cast the film.

The main star, Nanook, is indeed a hunter, and we see him harpooning a seal, wrestling with a walrus, and building remarkable igloos. But his loving wives and adorable children weren't his own. Flaherty staged the family and their activities to capture Inuit life. But he exaggerated the remoteness and the pre-modern qualities of their daily lives.

Flaherty was open about this, and his staged scenes mesmerized audiences nonetheless. It seems that Flaherty avoided the cinestance problem by recruiting actors to film scenes of daily activities and family life in an igloo.

The Ax Fight

Flaherty's approach to visually recording and presenting Inuit life inspired countless documentary filmmakers, among many anthropologists. One instance: Napoleon Chagnon and his film partner Timothy Asch left a camera on during a fight they witnessed among a band of South American forest dwellers.

They edited the footage into an anthropological film titled *The Ax Fight*, which is now shown in hundreds of anthropology classes every year. Unlike Flaherty, Chagnon and Asch didn't stage an ax fight with local actors. Instead, the camera just sits there, drawn on a confusing scene.

The year was 1971, and Chagnon and Asch had just arrived in their Amazonian host village. A fight broke out right before their eyes. An enduring tension in the community boiled over when visitors from a neighboring community asked to be fed despite their refusal to help out in their hosts' gardens.

Then, a male visitor beats a woman who has refused to give him food. Distraught, she screams and is comforted by family. Her brother and husband settle the dispute, first with clubs, and then with axes and machetes.

However, only 1 man is hurt, and there isn't much fighting because people intervene, placing themselves between the 2 groups.

Chagnon and Asch captured about 10 minutes of this half-hour episode. For their final film, they show the footage 4 times in a row.

- In the 1st version, they show an unedited version with sound. Some comments by the filmmakers as they were filming are audible, but there is no narration or explanation of what the viewer is seeing.
- In the 2nd version, Chagnon's voice explains what's happening, including his own original confusion about what was going on.
- In the 3rd version, the filmmakers diagram the lineages and families involved in the fight. This presentation makes it clear that the viewer is witnessing 1 episode of an enduring conflict.
- Finally, Changnon and Asch present an edited version of the fight, which transparently illustrates how the filmmakers' own cultural point of view is at work when they're making ethnographic films.

Their approach recognized that ethnographic filmmakers reveal culture at work on both sides of the lens. They dealt with that challenge through transparency. From raw footage and confusion to an edited episode that finally makes sense, Chagnon and Asch bring the viewer into their process before sharing their final version of events.

Jean Rouch

The ethnographic filmmaker Jean Rouch took the Chagnon and Asch approach to another level. Rouch did some amazing ethnographic film projects with the Dogon cliff dwellers in northern Mali. And he never lets the viewer forget that they're seeing a constructed scene. Specifically, he himself steps into the lens with his subjects, and he even shows film and equipment in his shots.

For the viewer and the participant, Rouch felt that cinestance was unavoidable. He decided to accept it and make it part of the story. His approach was a logical step toward what is now called participatory video and photography. Participatory visual approaches are quite common in anthropology today.

These ethnographic encounters place photography and video equipment into the hands of research populations themselves, who then visually reveal their attitudes and worldview with images instead of words.

Suggested Reading

Becker, *Art Worlds*.

Errington, *The Death of Authentic Primitive Art*.

Henley, *The Adventure of the Real*.

Marion and Crowder, *Visual Research*.

Questions to Consider

1. What is visual anthropology, and what kinds of work do visual anthropologists do?

2. How do social Darwinist ideas spill over into the way we categorize non-Western art?

3. What are some classic anthropology films, and how do they differ in terms of the way their filmmakers chose to document or present non-Western cultures?

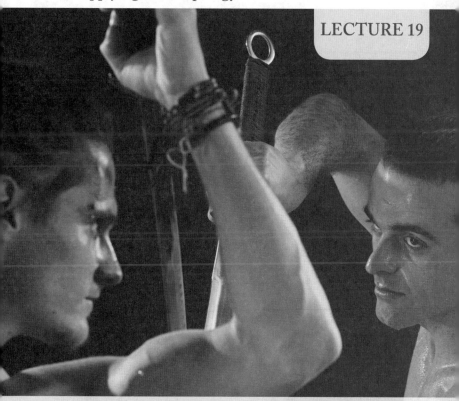

Conflict and Reconciliation across Cultures

F or the rest of this course, we'll see how anthropological perspectives contribute ideas and insight on some of the biggest challenges facing humankind. From war and conflict to criminal justice and health, anthropology has exciting contributions to share. This lecture focuses on violence and conflict resolution. In addition to uncovering the roots of violence, anthropology has important lessons to bring to the table when it comes to providing cross-cultural insight on conflict resolution.

Three Myths

Anthropology, with its 4-field approach, can clear up 3 major myths about humanity and our so-called violent nature. Myth 1 is that there has always been warfare. Myth 2 is that we are biologically predisposed to violence. Myth 3 is that warfare is universal.

Regarding myth 1: War is a recent development in our human history. *Homo sapiens* have been around for 200,000 years. But the archaeological record indicates that war, as we understand it today, only emerged some 10,000 years ago, around the advent of agriculture.

- Before agriculture, the survival of small hunter-gatherer groups required a level of cooperation that made conflict counterproductive for all parties. That's not to say that hunter-gatherers never fought, but these fights (or forager conflicts) rarely erupted into all-out war.

- Because non-sedentary people can't accumulate property the way Westerners do today, they cultivated communal lifestyles. In fact, we can observe this lifestyle, even in contemporary hunter-gatherer societies.

- For example, anthropologist Marjorie Shostak lived among the San people of the Kalahari, and she recorded the life history of a remarkable woman named Nisa. Nisa's community taught her that feeding all bellies takes precedence over individual accumulation or surplus. Without a surplus or troves of private property, the incentive for war isn't eliminated, but it is greatly reduced.

- However, the agricultural revolution changed all that. Sedentary living and agricultural surplus sparked the inevitable rise of urban centers and empires. And that's where the archaeological record shows us a sharp increase in large-scale, organized violence or war.

- The 20th century, according to historian Eric Hobsbawm, was the most murderous in recorded history. Warfare took the lives of some 187 million people in the 20th century.

- At first, 20th-century warfare was essentially limited to inter-state conflict and civil wars. But now, in the 21st century, armed conflict is no longer in the exclusive hands of governments and states. In fact, 21st-century warfare permeates civilian lives.

- At the turn of the 20th century, only 5% of combat casualties, on average, were civilians. By the end of World War II, however, the tide turned. Around two-thirds of World War II casualties were civilian deaths.
- That figure has risen today to approximately 90%. That is to say, 90% of those who die in 21st-century war are civilians. Ultimately, warfare as we know it today is truly a modern phenomenon.

Now for myth 2, the idea that we are biologically predisposed to violence. Are we programmed for conflict? In some ways, it appears so. But there might be other biological factors at work that show us that we're not predestined for violence and war.

- In their book *Demonic Males*, Richard Wrangham and Dale Peterson show that chimpanzees, like some humans, beat, rape, and kill other chimpanzees.
- But this predilection of our chimpanzee cousins is not an inevitable dimension of our own biological being.

Around two-thirds of World War II casualties were civilian deaths.

Wrangham and Peterson remind us to look at bonobo apes too.

- Unlike the violence we see in chimpanzees and gorillas, bonobos are relatively peaceful. Bonobo males do occasionally become aggressive and violent, but they rarely kill or rape. Why? Tight-knit bands of female bonobos gang up on and attack male counterparts who act up.

- Regarding humans: Our propensity for conflict resolution may be every bit as powerful as any inclination to fight. The anthropologist Carolyn Nordstrom documented this phenomenon among humans in her civil war ethnography: *Mozambique: A Different Kind of War Story*.

- Nordstrom looked deeper into unfathomable violence and aggression of 15 years of war. She described soldiers, wartime profiteers, and ordinary people. Remarkably, she revealed a propensity for cooperation among ordinary people in the face of extraordinary violence.

- Ordinary people created ways to actively socialize combatants back into a life of nonviolence. They established a network of healers, and they even kidnapped and reconditioned soldiers toward nonviolence.

- It's apparent that there are some biological mechanisms at work in the history of human warfare. But we're equally or perhaps more inclined toward making peace.

Now for the 3rd myth: the idea that war is universal. There are people in the human family tree who make peace seem as inevitable as war.

- The Amish, for example, refuse to fight in wars. They don't even take disputes to court unless all internal efforts to resolve a conflict have failed. One of the core Amish beliefs is the doctrine of non-resistance.

- Similarly, India's Jain religion sees the path to peace as our ultimate purpose. Ascetic Jain monks even go to the extreme of sweeping a path as they walk, to avoid stepping on small unsuspecting insects. Jains practice peace by fostering goodwill toward

The Amish refuse to fight in wars.

others, based on the unity and sanctity of all life.

- Another example: The San of the Kalahari region are super-sharers. They're one of the oldest indigenous populations on earth, tracing their cultural history back some 20,000 years. They are known as peaceful people who discourage fighting, aggression, and even competition.

Conflict Resolution: Mali

This lecture will now look at some cross-cultural examples of conflict resolution strategies to see how people transcend violence and aggression elsewhere in the world.

Once a thriving global empire, today the Republic of Mali suffers from extreme poverty and a complex security crisis that may take decades to repair. But thousands of rural Malian villages show 2 terrific daily practices that foster peace over conflict.

One example is joking cousins. Take the example of the Sangare and Doumbia families. These families have exchanged friendly insults and laughs for generations. Every family name in

Mali has a joking cousin alliance. Anthropologists interpret this cultural phenomenon as a safety valve preventing enduring social conflict.

Another safety valve that promotes unity over conflict is the village meeting. The meeting protocol itself is an act of consensus building: If someone's making a request, that request is passed up and down the line of village elders, repeated until everyone has had the opportunity to add their voice to the discussion.

Conflict Resolution: Liberia

In West Africa in Liberia, the Kpelle people use a conflict resolution practice that they call the Kpelle moot. The Kpelle are more interested in reconciliation rather than retribution-style justice. When an offense threatens the social harmony within a Kpelle village, the entire community comes together to hold a moot.

The moot forum takes place in someone's home rather than a courthouse. The complainant who calls for the moot selects a family member to serve as a mediator, but there's no singular judge or jury. In the moot, everyone chimes in.

The conflicting parties directly question and challenge each other. The mediator and the audience all join in. By the end of this long discussion, the person deemed at fault publicly apologizes and presents a small gift or two to the aggrieved. The aggrieved, in turn, offers a smaller gift to help repair the relationship.

Anthropologists attribute this form of reconciliatory justice as unique for small-scale societies. In a small, rural, cooperative community, people simply can't afford enduring conflict. It undermines the social harmony required to make a living off the land. The Kpelle moot vets justice while maintaining the social network that ensures the village's bellies will remain full.

Anthropology in the Military

In Afghanistan, the US military has used anthropology to better understand the sociocultural dimensions of Afghan communities. Anthropology in the military is not new, but not everyone agrees that this is a good idea.

In the 1960s, the US government launched Project Camelot, based at American University. Project Camelot was a counterinsurgency study led by anthropologists and other social and behavioral scientists.

The logic was that US national security was threatened by insurgencies throughout the world, particularly in neighboring Latin America. The orchestrators of Project Camelot brought in some anthropology because insurgencies signaled a breakdown of social order, and the military wanted to better understand the social and cultural processes that lead to these transformative events.

Shortly after collaborating Latin American scholars discovered the true purpose and funding source, the military shut down the program. But evidence shows that similar work continued nonetheless.

Prominent anthropologists like Margaret Mead and Marshall Sahlins were so affronted by this military coopting of anthropology, particularly in Latin American and in Southeast Asia, that they helped pass a stern resolution by the American Anthropological Association (AAA).

Simply put, they made it clear that anthropologists should not participate in what they labeled "clandestine" intelligence work.

In 2007, the American Anthropology Association once again spoke up about the militarization of anthropology. Specifically, they were reacting to a new military project operating in Afghanistan. It was called the Human Terrain System (HTS).

The 2007 statement was clear that the HTS violated the AAA code of ethics, which mandates that anthropologists do no harm to research subjects. Unlike previous militarized applications of anthropology, the HTS teams put anthropologists in actual warzone combat units. They could carry weapons alongside other, more conventionally trained soldiers.

The goal, however, was for the anthropologists to help soldiers and local populations communicate and understand each other. One example would be the Jirga. The Jirga, a community's council of elders, was a setting in which community members build consensus with guidance and discussion of Muslim values and teachings.

Anthropologists helped the US military recognize the importance of these civic conversations. They brought combat units and communities together. They won friends through understanding and collaborative social projects like building schools, or helping the elders deal with problems ranging from food scarcity to fears of being attacked.

The primary rationale for deploying HTS teams in Iraq and Afghani war zones was to curtail casualties by winning the hearts and minds of local communities. And to an extent, they did. But the program quickly faltered after critiques of mismanagement and dubious behavior along with a serious challenge by professional anthropologists across the nation.

In reaction to the HTS program, the AAA made it clear they were concerned by the fact that anthropologists were working in combat units. Specifically, critics questioned the voluntary subject's ability to "decline" participation in HTS anthropology work, owing to the presence of weapons.

Similarly, if any of the information warzone anthropologists produce

is used by the military for the purpose of designing combat campaigns and identifying potential targets, then the participating anthropologists are in clear violation of their code of ethics. Their work directly alters the winds of war, and this can undermine the work of all anthropologists abroad. The last thing a field researcher needs is to be accused of being a meddling intelligence officer.

At its peak, the HTS employed some 500 people, who served in 30 teams deployed in both Iraq and Afghanistan. The cost: $725 million. But once the majority of US troops were pulled out of these theaters, the HTS program was officially closed in 2014.

However, it's likely we'll see new forms of anthropology in combat zones and elsewhere in the military. Despite the controversy, the generic idea of a military with cultural knowledge of the people they engage with has become essential.

Suggested Reading

Little and Smith, *Mayas in Postwar Guatemala*.

Nordstrom, *A Different Kind of War Story*.

Peterson and Wrangham, *Demonic Males*.

Price, *Weaponizing Anthropology*.

Questions to Consider

1. What are two specific examples of how people across cultures work together to reduce conflict?

2. Are humans biologically predisposed toward war and violence?

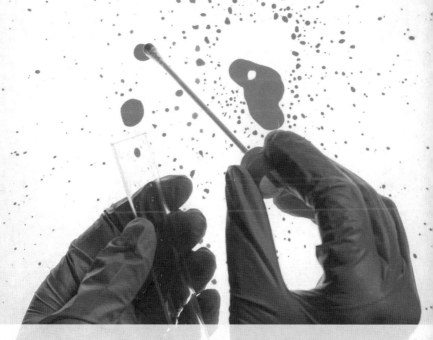

Forensics and Legal Anthropology

A nthropology is not just an intellectual exercise that satisfies our curiosity about human cultures, past and present. It's also a discipline that can give us practical insight into some of the biggest challenges we face as our planet's 21ˢᵗ-century caretakers. This lecture expands on that theme by looking at the fascinating topics of forensics and legal anthropology. Forensic anthropologists essentially analyze and identify unknown human remains, among other things. They do so for legal, criminal justice, and humanitarian purposes.

A Hypothetical Discovery

By studying skeletal remains, forensic anthropologists can determine a victim's age, sex, ancestry, health, and more. Perhaps most importantly, they can determine identity and cause of death.

Let's walk through the basic process that a forensic anthropologist would go through to determine a victim's biological profile and cause of death. Imagine we're in New Mexico. A construction crew on the Turquoise Trail in Cerrillos just unearthed a rather grim discovery: a battered box containing an assortment of what appears to be human bones.

Once the bones are in hand, it's off to the lab. We inventory what we have as we lay them out on a table in their respective anatomical positions. Specifically, we determine that these are indeed human bones.

Next, we work out whether we have 1 or more individuals here. For our hypothetical remains, the bone ratios point toward there being just 1 individual.

Finally, we figure out whether we have a male or a female here. The pelvis is the best indicator for biological sex for 3 reasons:

- The pelvic brim—the hollowed-out ring inside the pelvis—is heart shaped in males but more circular in females.
- The sacrum is the tip of the tailbone. Here, a forensic anthropologist would look to see if it points more inward or outward. If the sacrum is pointing inward, the specimen is a male.
- The pubic angle or arch is the outside angle created by the bottom front of the pelvis. If the pubic arch is less than 90 degrees wide, that indicates a male. Arches greater than 90 degrees are indicative of a female pelvis.

Now for our hypothetical discovery: Let's say we examine the remains and discern a heart-shaped pelvis with an inward-pointing sacrum and a pubic arch under 90 degrees. The conclusion: We're looking at a male.

Alternatively, we can usually work out biological sex simply by examining the skull. Just like the pelvis, there's sexual dimorphism in human skulls:

- Male skulls tend to have square-shaped chins. A female skull will have a more rounded, almost pointed chin.
- The back of the jaw is also an indicator: On males, we'll see more of a 90-degree angle, versus the female's wider Angle.
- Another feature that can help discern the biological sex of human remains is the orbital margin—or eye sockets. If we look to the top edge of the socket, we see the supraorbital margin or

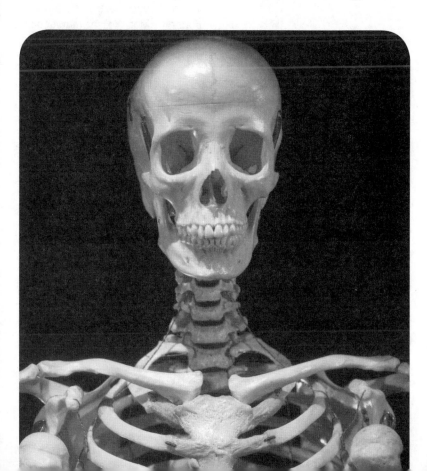

edge. In females, this edge is sharper. In males, we see more rounded upper edges, with larger brow ridges and a more sloped forehead. By comparing a specimen with established comparative measures, we can accurately determine biological sex most of the time.

Returning to our hypothetical victim: The chin, jaw, and orbital margins all confirm what we concluded from the pelvis. We have a male.

Aging the Remains

But what was his age at death? Here again, the skull can help us. Skulls have sutures that join the bones of the skull, and as we age, they begin to fuse. Going straight down the middle of the skull is the sagittal suture, which fuses between the ages of 29–35. On our hypothetical skull, the sagittal suture is about halfway fused. We can conclude that the male was in his early 30s.

How long has he been dead? To figure this out, we "read" insects. Some insects arrive right away and get right to the corpse. Insects like blowflies or maggots can be present for a few days to a year or more. Seeing where blowflies are in their development cycle can help us get an accurate date of death down to the day.

For our hypothetical human remains, those "early" insects are long gone. These bones are at least a couple years old, and probably older. We'll have to send them out for some further testing.

Forensic Anthropology

Forensic anthropology has a comprehensive protocol and toolkit to work out the details we need to assemble a profile for unidentified human remains. In our hypothetical lab, we got a great start with just a few quick procedures: We definitely have a male in his early 30s who died at least a couple years ago.

Forensic specialists can bring new tools: forensic archaeology, DNA analysis, chemical dating techniques, and so on. There are even dental, pollen, geological, and isotope analysis. Isotope analysis is a fascinating technique that can even be used to reconstruct the diet of prehistoric peoples.

Forensic anthropologists work in a wide variety of occupations and settings. Many forensic anthropologists work as professors and academic researchers, but most of them work outside of academia in government agencies, the armed forces, medical examiner's offices, and more.

Following the catastrophic loss of life in tragedies like the 9/11 terrorist attacks, forensic anthropology has taken on a new humanitarian dimension. Forensic anthropologists have increasingly been called on when it comes time for identifying victims in mass-casualty events.

We can also see the growing importance of forensic anthropology through the lens of the US Congress. In the 1990s, 2 important pieces of federal legislation were passed—and they both demonstrate the broad social role that forensic anthropologists are playing outside of the academy.

- One is the Native American Graves Protection and Repatriation Act, or NAGPRA. Passed in 1990, NAGPRA

requires that the remains of any Native Americans, once discovered, be turned over to the appropriate contemporary Native American nation. This protection covers gravesites and artifacts, not just human remains.

- In 1996, the Aviation Disaster Family Assistance Act was signed into law. This act basically formalized a federal infrastructure aimed specifically at dealing with the aftermath of mass casualties. This infrastructure supports and dispatches DMORT units, or Disaster Mortuary Operational Response Teams.

- These teams include forensic anthropologists and a host of other experts. There are funeral directors, medical examiners, pathologists, medical records experts, fingerprint specialists, forensic dentists, X-ray technicians, and more.

- Following a string of airline accidents, the first DMORT team was launched in the 1990s. The role of forensic anthropology was integrated into the DMORT system, specifically for identifying remains in humanitarian service to the deceased and their families.

Anthropologist Snapshot: Mary Manhein

Mary Manhein is a gifted storyteller and an honored member of the prestigious American Academy of Forensic Sciences. She is the archetype of the forensic anthropologist. In her career, she handled over 1000 forensic cases, and was called upon by law enforcement agencies from all over the US.

Notably, she was a critical force in establishing the Louisiana Repository for Unidentified and Missing Persons Information Program. This program brings closure to case after case of unidentified and missing persons in Louisiana.

Manhein has been an active DMORT team member for years. Her notable cases have ranged from Hurricane Katrina to serial killers. One of her toughest cases was the recovery of 7 astronauts following the *Columbia* space shuttle disaster in 2003. The account of this surreal experience is a standout chapter in her book, *Trail of Bones*.

Anthropologist Snapshot: Gillian Fowler

Another major figure in this field is Gillian Fowler. Fowler took up forensic anthropology after hearing horrific stories told by Guatemalan refugees in Mexico. The refugees had fled a civil war that claimed some 200,000 lives.

Fowler happened to be teaching English in Mexico when these stories compelled her to get a degree in forensic archaeology and eventually to head to Guatemala. There, she spent 6 years exhuming mass graves.

She was determined to help families find loved ones who were taken away and never seen again. Their experience of loss without closure had gone on for over 2 decades. But Fowler's efforts helped change that.

The healing nature of this work was evident in Fowler's lab where victim's families actually visited their skeletal remains. Fowler's account mentions family members laying flowers, lighting candles, praying, and crying.

The candles and flowers in Fowler's lab are clear signs that the power

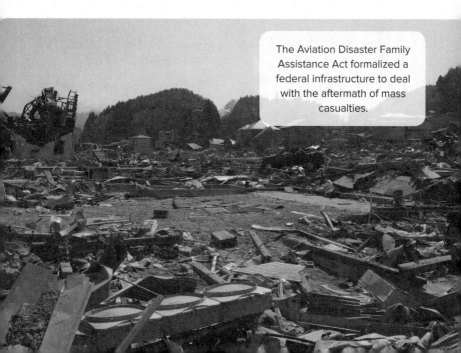

The Aviation Disaster Family Assistance Act formalized a federal infrastructure to deal with the aftermath of mass casualties.

of forensic anthropology extends beyond legal and criminal cases. Forensic anthropology has a critical, deeply effective, humanitarian purpose. Furthermore, the data that forensic anthropology produces has been used in criminal courts to successfully prosecute many of the leaders responsible for mass killings.

Suggested Reading

Clarke, *Fictions of Justice*.

Ferllini, *Silent Witness*.

Manhein, *The Bone Lady*.

Steadman, *Hard Evidence*.

Questions to Consider

1. How is it that forensic anthropologists can actually examine unidentified human remains, even if all that remains is a skull and/or pelvis?

2. How and why has the work of forensic anthropologists integrated a new "humanitarian" focus in the 21st and late 20th centuries?

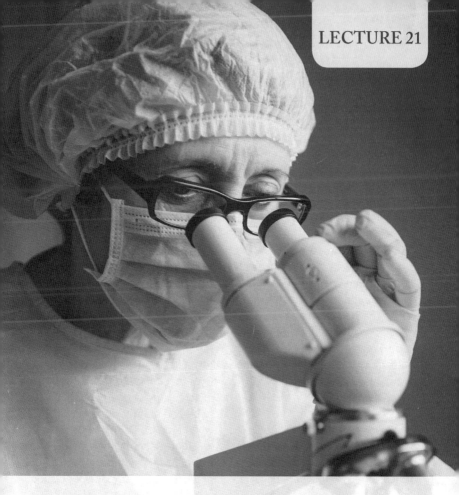

Medical Anthropology

This lecture discusses one of the largest specialization areas in contemporary anthropology: medical anthropology. Contemporary medical anthropology is a definitive example of applied anthropology. From an interdisciplinary, 4-field approach, medical anthropologists chart the depths of the biology-culture nexus of human health and healing. The central ethos of medical anthropology is inspired by the idea that human health (good and bad) is much more than biology.

The Nocebo Effect and Medical Anthropology

Researchers who study the nocebo effect—damage caused by negative thoughts—essentially look at the various ways that our thoughts can harm us. A recent study showed the sheer power of thought on human heath.

In this nocebo study, patients were given sugar water and told that it would induce vomiting. A full 80% vomited upon drinking that sugar water. The power of the brain and what we think can definitely impact our biological health. Therefore, we'd do well to understand what's going on with this body-mind connection.

That's one of the reasons medical anthropology emerged in the first place. Doctors and other health professionals, long aware of the placebo and nocebo effect, increasingly recognized that illness and health aren't exclusively biological.

Because anthropologists are equally at home with biology and culture, anthropology emerged as a great way to think about medicine and health beyond, yet inclusive of, our biology.

Malaria

About half the world's population is vulnerable to malaria. Hundreds of thousands of people die of malaria every year. It's a disease that not only kills people, but also drains households of the critical labor they need to keep bellies full throughout the year.

Malaria is caused by certain blood parasites that are carried and transmitted by mosquitos, so having malaria is definitely a biological event. But it's also much more.

Malaria used to be a major public health issue in the United States. Prior to the mid-20th century, malaria crippled the nation's labor force and military. For example, when Franklin D. Roosevelt signed the Tennessee Valley Authority into law, malaria affected almost a third of the Tennessee Valley population.

In World War II, the US lost somewhere around 60,000 soldiers to malaria. In the 1940s, the military enacted the Malaria Control in War Areas program. A few years later, that was transformed into the Communicable Disease Center. Today, it is the CDC, or the Centers for Disease Control and Prevention.

The initial campaign against malaria was nothing short of remarkable. With the widespread application of DDT, the CDC partnered with state and local health agencies in 13 states. And starting in 1947, they commenced spraying millions of homes, and with stunning results. In less than 5 years, the CDC completed its job. Malaria and reports of malaria infections were eliminated from the US.

Most Americans will never experience malaria in their lifetimes. But the eradication of the disease in the US was not a question of human biology at work. Without the collective action and organized campaigns of the 1940s, malaria would still be endemic in the US. Rather than biological adaptations or vaccines, the economy and political history of the US wiped malaria out.

"Pocahontas Goes to the Clinic"

A great example of medical anthropology in action is a piece by Cheryl Mattingly called "Pocahontas Goes to the Clinic." Mattingly took her medical anthropology to a clinic. Her work showed that biomedicine is most effective when it's paired with cultural understanding and competence. In her study, she revealed how cultural misunderstanding undermines the quest for positive health outcomes.

One of her examples involves sickle cell anemia patients, particularly black teenage males. Mattingly documented how black teen males with sickle cell anemia are often mislabeled as "med-seekers."

With regular hospital visits for pain treatment, the sociocultural context of being a black teenager in the US carries the additional burden of being labeled a troublesome med-seeker, when in fact these kids need medical treatment.

Another angle from Mattingly's study featured Spiderman. Mattingly described a boy who was neutralized by fear of medical personnel and equipment. Doctors needed to test the boy's mobility to properly diagnose and treat him, but he was nonresponsive.

Mattingly explained that as soon as the attending physician found a common cultural frame through which to relate to this boy, everything changed. They assuaged the boy's fears and turned him into a compliant patient by talking about Spiderman. When the medical procedures were translated into superhero tests aimed at helping this young patient and his crime-fighting ambitions, the boy leaped into action.

Adequate biomedical treatment was made possible only after the boy jumped out of his shy demeanor. And that happened only because the physician built a cross-cultural bridge of understanding. Mattingly shows us with her vignettes that, along with technical prowess, we also need health professionals with strong cross-cultural skills.

Illness versus Disease

In medical anthropology, illness is defined as a cultural experience. For example, consider someone who is a diabetic. The illness is not diabetes. Illness is the person's subjective experience as a diabetic. Arthur Kleinmann, a foundational figure in medical anthropology, tells us that illness is an individual's "culture-bound understanding of the event."

It's the business of medical anthropology to separate the subjective experience of illness from the biological phenomenon of disease. Treating a disease is not the same as treating an illness. Disease requires a physician to fix what's going on in the body. But illness requires someone to fix what's going on in the patient's head—the subjective experience. Disease is not culture bound, but illness is.

As an example, take diabetes in the US versus Mali. Being a rural Malian diabetic is quite different from having this condition in the US. Namely, in rural Mali, one may not even be diagnosed as a diabetic. One might not even get tested for diabetes because their illness—their subjective health experience—could very likely be attributed to some other condition.

Even in the event of a diagnosis for a Malian, the treatment plan presents a number of complications. Many families have to scrape to buy a single dose of antibiotics, let alone a recurring expense for insulin injections. Even if the medicine, supplies, and test kits were made affordable, there may be no refrigeration or electricity for the insulin.

Health

Anthropologists need a precise yet inclusive definition of health. The World Health Organization (WHO) defines health as "complete

physical, mental, and social well-being." And they add that it involves "the capability to function in the face of changing circumstances."

The WHO also strives to promote the highest possible level of health so that people can live a "socially and economically productive life."

The WHO's definition of health clearly goes beyond mere biology. And this anthropological perspective is not coincidence. Medical anthropologists play a host of roles in the WHO and in related institutions throughout the world.

Case Study: Medical School

The rest of this lecture takes a look at 2 classic medical anthropology case studies. First up is a 1993 study by Byron J. Good and Mary-Jo DelVecchio Good. The Goods studied the peculiar culture of first-year students at Harvard Medical School.

One section of this study described the close and rather tender relationships that many medical students develop with their first cadavers and sometimes their surviving families. After spending

hours and hours with a cadaver, the students realize that the deceased's selfless gift is what opened the path to becoming a practicing physician.

Another observation from the study is that as medical students go through their first year, the experience literally changes the way they see the body. By breaking down the body into its constituent systems and components, the lab and lectures eventually render the complexity of the human body into a machine with working parts.

Case Study: *Flexible Bodies*

A second classic medical anthropology case study comes from anthropologist Emily Martin. In her 1994 book, *Flexible Bodies*, Martin delves deep into the collective American psyche to learn about how non-physicians understand the immune system.

Martin did a comprehensive field study at 3 sites. She worked at an immunology research lab. She volunteered at a house for HIV-positive individuals. And she also worked as an AIDS activist. In all, she did some 200 interviews, along with untold pages of field notes from her day-to-day observations.

Martin shows that the metaphors we use reveal a lot about how we understand our immune system. Specifically, she showed that in the US, militarism is a common metaphor for medicine and treating disease. We *fight* cavities and *battle* cancer.

But ultimately, Emily Martin's study shows that in the US, people are shifting from militaristic, fortress-based metaphors for the body and health. Instead, from the age of AIDS onward, she sees our metaphors focusing more on dynamism and flexibility.

As they entered the 21st century, Martin says, Americans were no longer focusing on the idea of the immune system as a battle-ready army of white blood cells. Rather, they were coming to see and value adaptability in the immune system. This new focus on flexibility has broader cultural ramifications, including openness to new ways of treating disease and maintaining our health.

Suggested Reading

Brown and Closser, *Understanding and Applying Medical Anthropology*.

Packard, *The Making of a Tropical Disease*.

Wilkinson and Kleinmann, *A Passion for Society*.

Questions to Consider

1. What's the difference between illness and disease, and why do medical anthropologists underscore these differences?

2. In the hospital, in what ways might cultural differences or misunderstandings result in making you sicker?

3. How do anthropologists contribute to working out global health challenges?

Anthropology and Economic Development

International development has been a cornerstone of anthropological inquiry for many decades. Development anthropology, as a specialization, puts anthropologists on the front lines of international development. Development anthropologists bring their research to bear on socioeconomic, cultural, ecological, and technical problems around the world. They collaborate with knowledge experts and communities in search of practical solutions to human problems. This lecture takes a close look at development anthropology.

Robert Redfield

When it comes to the theoretical origins of development anthropology, the best place to start is probably with Robert Redfield. Redfield was instrumental in shaping a subfield known as peasant studies, a term that has evolved into the anthropology of development.

His research approach reinforced the 4-field tradition that Franz Boas laid as the foundation of anthropology. He blended cultural studies, biology, linguistics, and archaeology to collect data on poor rural farming societies.

Redfield's career was launched by his work with Mexican immigrants in Chicago. Ruminating over the fact that these immigrants had lives in both the US and Mexico, his focus turned to what life is truly like in rural Mexican societies.

He went to Mexico in 1926 and 1928 with hopes of finding the perfect community to study a poor rural farming society. He found that community in Tepoztlán, a small agricultural community of family farmers.

It was here that Redfield developed 2 of his core concepts: the idea of the peasantry and the idea of the little community.

Redfield says the peasantry is a category of pre-urban human society. Peasant society has a few requisite traits.

- First, peasants eat what they grow. They are farmers.
- Second, peasants don't treat land as capital or commodity. Instead they follow traditional land-tenure systems, which can vary across cultures. In one Malian village, for example, families maintain their farming territory over the generations, only so long as they continue to cultivate them.
- Third, a peasant society is rather powerless against the greater forces that surround it. Finally, the peasantry lives in rural territory that is linked to the rest of the world through regional market towns.

Redfield created the idea of the little community to help us grasp what life is like among the peasantry.

According to the work of Robert Redfield, a peasant society is rather powerless against the greater forces that surround it.

The little community, says Redfield, represents an "earlier" form of human society. It is small and culturally homogenous. And daily life in the little community is structured by age- and sex-based groups.

Another characteristic of the little community is that things largely stay the same. One generation follows the next, living and working the same basic lives. A final trait: The little community is self-sufficient as an organic whole. In other words, the little community takes care of its people from birth to death.

Redfield taught that the little community was an essential unit of analysis for development anthropology around the world. He promoted participant observation as essential. For him, embedded, participant observation was the only way to get at a community's essence.

Lewis and Mintz

Redfield inspired new questions for a new generation of anthropologists. One of these scholars was Oscar Lewis. Lewis revisited Tepoztlán, and in 1951, he published a revised account. His primary departure from Redfield was that, for him, the little community was not a complete picture.

Per Lewis, the little community wasn't the primordially harmonious society that Redfield portrayed. And it wasn't a self-sustaining community. Instead, it was tied to a complex network of regional and global forces.

Another anthropologist who built on Redfield's work was Sidney Mintz. His methodological innovation was to use anthropology to study commodities instead of communities.

And this innovation has become a central thread in contemporary development anthropology. By examining coffee and sugar, for example, anthropological inquiry can now reveal the ties that Lewis identified as connecting little communities with the rest of the world. Mintz's groundbreaking history of sugar, *Sweetness and Power*, has become a foundational text across fields like the social sciences, history, ethnic studies, and international business.

The Mission

Development anthropology's mission has 3 components:

1. Development anthropologists must embrace their role as agents of social change.
2. Development anthropologists should apply their unique, 4-field approach and their specializations to produce empirical and comprehensive development studies.
3. Based on empirical field studies, development anthropologists should produce collective theories of development.

Theories of development are not the exclusive domain of anthropologists. But most development anthropologists work within a common framework of ideas called development theory.

Development theory is dynamic, which means we can trace the evolution of certain key concepts within the overarching framework. One of the most influential—and unfortunate—of these concepts is the idea of the so-called third world.

An alternate term is *majority world*. After all, the third world's population is clearly the majority. They're not some distant, disconnected population.

The pervasive, deceptive term *third world* dates back to author Alfred Sauvy, who coined the term *tiers monde*, or third world, in 1952. From his Cold War perspective, Sauvy identified the third world as unallied regions that had yet to fully realize the capitalist model of the United States (the first world), nor the socialist vision of the Soviet Union (the second world). Instead, these countries and their populations were territorial battlegrounds for the Cold War.

Today's Order

The global economic order we're familiar with in the 21st century has shallow roots that go back to 1944 in Bretton Woods, New Hampshire.

Emerging as a victor from both World Wars, the US had escaped the monstrous carnage of war-torn Europe and Asia. As such, its relative power rose as the US worked with the international community to organize and finance the rebuilding of the world and the modern global economy.

At the Bretton Woods Conference, representatives from allied nations brokered the development for what became the International Monetary Fund and the World Bank. The idea was that the global economy would shift from the gold standard to the US dollar. Those countries with surplus would contribute funds that would be provided to countries that were struggling with deficits.

The trouble is the strings attached to taking money from the World Bank. For starters, such money is a loan, and loans have interest. In addition, countries have to follow these rules:

1. A country must agree to reduce existing budgets by cutting subsidies and social services across the board.
2. A country must eliminate trade and investment restrictions to spur exports and industry.
3. A country must devaluate the local currency.

During the boom years of 1945–1969, this approach appeared to have some success. But since then, things haven't been so rosy. Global poverty endures, and arguably the system that emerged out of Bretton Woods undermines peace in our time.

So what happened? Anthropologists came to realize their principles of international development weren't as universal and objective as once believed.

Changes

Development theory changed over the course of the 20th century and into the 21st century. One way to examine this is through the modernization school. The modernization school asserts an evolutionary schema that places all the world economies on a continuum from traditional to modern. This theory is attributed to Walt Rostow, who articulated the 5 stages of economic growth.

The first of Rostow's 5 stages is the traditional, collective economy, which corresponds well with Redfield's idea of the little community.

The way out of this "primitive" state is to enter the stage Rostow refers to as the preconditions for takeoff. In this early phase, a society works out solutions for economic growth, but they're unsustainable.

Then, with some careful planning and external investment, a country can move up to what Rostow calls the takeoff stage, where resistance to steady growth is finally overcome.

For the modernization school, a "takeoff" economy is defined by the 10% rule. That means that the investment and savings rate rises to around 10%. As industry grows, more and more income is reinvested.

Once an emerging economy achieves take off, it evolves into to the drive to maturity. Rostow notes that this is the stage that economic growth finally becomes automatic.

That automatic, supposedly inevitable growth leads to the pinnacle of economic development: the age of high mass consumption. Ultimately, modernization theory is all about getting traditional farming societies to become high-consumption societies.

That's right in line with 19th-century anthropology, an era dominated by the widespread presumption that Western cultures were the biological and cultural pinnacle of human evolution. Anthropologists eventually grew critical of this presumption, and they updated their anthropological perspective of development.

Critiques of modernization began to emerge in the 1960s and '70s. Scholar Andre Gunder Frank was one of several theorists who represented the post-modernization phase of development theory: dependency theory.

Frank and dependency theorists pointed out the inconsistencies of modernization theory. They presented the world economy as an exploitative network of metropolis-satellite relationships. And the cards are stacked against so-called third world countries. They can't feasibly replicate the immeasurably costly arc that established the modern global economy. For example, Africa cannot enslave a foreign population to build a continental infrastructure for a new millennium.

Underdevelopment

Another brand of dependency theory is known as underdevelopment. This variation on dependency theory asserts that modernization actually produces under-developed societies.

Scholar and activist Walter Rodney wrote a book entitled *How Europe Underdeveloped Africa*, in which he eviscerated modernization theory. Rodney examined the socioeconomic, historical, and cultural dynamics of the developing world, and he documented how development programs in the modernization tradition actually produced underdevelopment.

He provided evidence for the colonial and postcolonial decline in status of women in developing countries. He also pointed out that conventional development schemes of the West invested in places like Africa for the purpose of resource extraction, which produced pockets of development. There are schools, roads, and health clinics in the third world, but they're not universal.

Development Today

How does development theory align with development practice in the 21st century? Development anthropologists may debate the specifics of development initiatives, but Redfield's instruction to embrace their role as agents for social change binds them.

The UN monitors real-world indicators like school enrollment numbers for girls.

Development anthropologists are serving in government and nongovernment positions focused on articulating and achieving a global standard for international development.

Today, this standard is largely reflected in the Millennium Development Goals (MDGs), which were adopted by the United Nations in 2000. These are a set of 8 goals that aim to reduce and then eliminate extreme poverty across the world in 1 generation.

The UN is measuring progress on 8 vectors. For example, the third MDG promotes gender equality. To measure country-by-country progress on this goal, the UN monitors real-world indicators like school enrollment numbers for girls and women's representation in national parliaments.

With tangible measurements like this over time, maybe it's not such a far-fetched idea that we might eventually eradicate extreme poverty and hunger across the globe.

Suggested Reading

Mintz, *Sweetness and Power*.

Nolan, *Development Anthropology*.

Redfield, *The Little Community and Peasant Society and Culture*.

Rodney, *How Europe Underdeveloped Africa*.

Questions to Consider

1. What is the role of the anthropologist in international development? How has that role changed (or has it changed) since Robert Redfield and the early days of development anthropology?

2. What is the theory of underdevelopment, and why does it take an anthropological perspective to see it?

Cultural Ecology

C ultural ecology examines the complex relations between people and their environment. Anthropologists using this approach distinguish themselves with their collective adherence to 2 big cultural ecology ideas. First, they argue that the natural environment sets certain possibilities from which people and cultures may choose. Second, naturally inspired possibilities and the element of human choice challenge the idea of environmental determinism, or the idea that cultural differences are environmentally determined. Rather than environmental determinism, cultural ecology asserts environmental "possibilism."

Julian Steward

Julian Steward finished his Anthropology Ph.D. in 1929 at the University of California, Berkeley, under the tutelage of Alfred Kroeber. Steward taught at a handful of universities, but for a decade in the midst of his career, he applied his talents to the Bureau of American Ethnology (BAE).

Established by Congress in 1879, the BAE's mission was to collect and curate all records and materials relating to Native Americans. The BAE had the task of bringing those records and programs to the Smithsonian Institution, which opened the National Museum of the American Indian 125 years later in 2004.

Steward was an excellent choice for the BAE because he had a rather unique approach to anthropology. Steward was not an empirical purist, but he did privilege environmental factors and the collection of material artifacts over the use of human informants.

He understood cultural evolution as multilineal: All cultures are on their own path. He explained that no singular force determines the course of cultural evolution. Rather, factors like the environment, economy, social organization, political system, technology, and ideologies influence cultural evolutionism.

One of Steward's most-replicated anthropological approaches was to empirically examine human societies by focusing on what he called its culture core. He advised would-be field researchers to investigate subsistence strategies within a culture. His idea was that as these dynamic strategies evolve over time, those changes would influence other cultural features like language and social organization.

Cultural Ecology Methods

In the 1950s, cultural ecology remained close to Steward's approach. It focused on investigating and documenting the intersection of culture, technology, environment, and human behavior.

But in the 1960s, there began to emerge an ecosystem approach, as illustrated by the work of Robert Netting. This new layer added concepts like caloric expenditure and the carrying capacity of human habitats.

Moving further into the century, Steward's student, Marvin Harris, took his teacher's methods to the extreme, presuming that all cultural elements stem from human adaptations to environmental pressures.

This extreme materialist explanation for cultural evolution elicited heated debates from the growing numbers of more interpretivist and postmodern anthropologists of the late 20th century. Nonetheless, Steward remains a seminal influence on the way we understand culture change and the dynamic relationship between culture and environment.

Robert Netting's Work

Inspired by Steward's work on Great Basin hunter-gatherer societies in North America, Robert Netting took off for some field research of his own to see if Steward's ecological approach would work for a small-scale agricultural society.

His project led to the 1968 ethnography *Hill Farmers of Nigeria*. In this terrific cultural ecology classic, Netting documented some brilliant farmers in northern Nigeria who cultivated terraced fields year-round using organic fertilizers like manure and compost.

Terrace fields

Netting reinforced core elements of cultural ecology. First and foremost, he opposed cultural and environmental determinism. Netting focused mainly on quantitative data. Rather than exploring the inner lives and folklore of his study community, he liked to hone in on the things he could observe and measure, like the farming calendar, tools, and diet.

Through a comparative historical approach, married with empiricism and cross-cultural perspectives, Netting emerged as a champion of the small-scale farmer.

Marvin Harris's Work

Marvin Harris doubled down on Steward's empiricism. In fact, he went as far as taking Steward's environmental possibilism into strict environmental determinism.

Harris argued that our sociocultural lives arise out of our subsistence practices. In essence, he said that all aspects of culture, from our mode of production to religion and ideology, originate from the way we eek out a living from the surrounding environment. His book, *Our Kind*, discusses scores of cultures from all over the world.

Harris was a brilliant raconteur who was a master at drawing cross-cultural connections. But his work was different from people like Julian Steward. Harris, by focusing exclusively on the material lives of his subjects, eschewed subjective accounts and human informants.

Instead, he stuck to the material world. In his famous piece on the sacred cattle of India, he laid bare his approach. If asked why so many Indians refuse to eat cows, many locals would say that cattle are sacred and must not be slaughtered for human feed.

But there's not a scientific measure for the sacredness of cows. As such, Harris rejects this explanation. He argued there are other, deeper, things afoot.

Rather than interviewing people, Harris analyzed preexisting quantitative data. He didn't even go to India. Instead, he crunched some numbers and revealed that the sacred cow may be more of an economic taboo rather than a religious one. In short, he showed how cattle are far more valuable alive than butchered.

Marvin Harris showed how cattle are far more valuable alive than butchered.

In the Indian economy, cattle are more valuable as producers of milk, offspring, and dung, rather than ground beef and steak cutlets. Cattle dung, for example, is used as organic fertilizer or fuel for cooking.

Harris wasn't arguing against religious explanations for this taboo. But he was demonstrating that religious explanations, and all other cultural elements, have deep roots in our material and productive lives.

Harris and his approach are connected to cultural ecology in the Julian Steward tradition, but his strict materialist perspective was a sharp diversion that eventually required its own name. Harris branded his theory and methods cultural materialism.

Cultural Materialism

Cultural materialism explains how the political, economic, domestic, ideological, and symbolic dimensions of society are ultimately rooted in how we meet our basic biological needs. Here's the basic methodology:

1. Focus on the observable and quantifiable.
2. When researching, embrace the scientific method. Develop methods and analyze

empirical data in testable and correctable ways. Methods and analysis must be replicable.

3. Using empirical data, reduce cultural phenomena like religion or political organization into observable, measurable variables for cross-cultural comparisons.

Harris's pyramid of cultural materialism provides a look at this approach.

1. Humans need to satisfy their basic human needs. That is the base of the pyramid, the infrastructure. For example, humans on Baffin Island would be wise to work out how to build shelters, fish, and hunt. Regarding reproduction: With limited resources, this island isn't capable of hosting large urban-level populations. Instead, they'll keep their population small yet viable.

2. The next level of the cultural pyramid is the structure. The structure level is where humans take care of their domestic and political economies. The domestic economy includes how people

The history of development anthropology clearly suggests that globalization generally weakens traditional knowledge.

organize families, gender and age roles, and kinship. The political economy is where people work out things like class structure, political organization, and trade.

3. The apex of the pyramid is the superstructure. With their basic needs met and political and domestic economies in place, people can turn to cultural elements like art, literature, music, dance, rituals, religion, science, and more.

Ironically, Harris and his cultural materialism outline the cultural diversity on our planet, only to reveal underlying structures that link directly back to our relative environments. Despite the surface-level diversity of the human family, Harris's cultural materialism pyramid shows that structurally, we're all the same. We're not different; our environments are.

Freelisting

Freelisting is an anthropology research method that opens new ways to for us to investigate the relationship between culture and environment. It's a text-analysis method.

Marsha Quinlan publishes widely on her freelist research, and she provides a great example of this method that is attuned to the ecological knowledge of rural Dominica.

She investigated local herbal medicine, and she wanted to see if local populations were losing generational knowledge on local medicinal plants. The history of development anthropology clearly suggests that globalization generally weakens traditional knowledge.

Quinlan interviewed her host community and asked them, one by one, to list all the local medicines they knew. This is freelisting. By getting these medicine lists from each respondent, she got a comprehensive view of every medicine this community knew.

Quinlan discovered some surprising results.

- She noticed that women knew more medicinal plants than men.
- Formal education was negatively associated with the number of medicinal plants people know. It seems that those who don't get a formal

education know more about medicinal plants.

- In sum, Quinlan discovered that globalization has complex effects on local knowledge systems. In the case of medicinal plant knowledge in Dominica, freelisting opened a window into the minds of her study community.

Through this method, her community taught her that prevailing ideas about the impact of globalization on local knowledge systems isn't as straightforward as once thought.

How Freelisting Works

Here's an example of how freelisting works: If Americans were asked to list all the animals they know, they'd likely have cats and dogs high on the list, but animals like emus and aardvarks would be less likely to appear.

When anthropologists collect and analyze these lists, they aggregate all the terms and sort them into 2 piles. One pile contains the popular terms; the rest of the terms go in the other pile. These piles are invaluable to anthropologists.

For example, an anthropologist could have people from a community freelist from the prompt "crops my family likes to grow." When the anthropologist aggregates those lists, the result will be an efficient snapshot of cultural consensus. It will be a master list of where there's consensus on the most important crops in this community as a whole.

The final, weighted results rank each term in the aggregate list based on both the popularity of each term—or the number of times it was listed—and the average rank of each term—or how high up it is on each list.

Anthropologists can also use freelist results to identify experts and other outliers within a culture. They can measure the similarity of each respondent to all other respondents, then plot the results so that 2 people with very similar results will show up as 2 dots next to each other.

Conversely, people who mention words that don't make everyone else's lists will have dots way off to the side. These people are either experts, or a little off, or don't fit within the cultural consensus for some other reason. Anthropologists go to the outliers for more information.

Cultural consensus modeling helps anthropologists examine how others see and organize their worlds. That's what makes it an ideal method for anthropologists like Quinlan who build upon the cultural ecology tradition.

Suggested Reading

Crawford, *Moroccan Households in the World Economy*.

Harris, *Good to Eat*.

Netting, *Smallholders, Householders*.

Steward, *Theory of Culture Change*.

Questions to Consider

1. What is cultural ecology, and how does it explain the complex relationship between people and their physical environment?

2. What are cultural consensus modeling and freelisting, and how do anthropologists use them to understand the ways different communities understand and manage their local ecology?

The Anthropology of Happiness

Throughout this course, we've seen how anthropology has emboldened our understanding of the complex layers that make us human. The course has looked at everything from our origins and biology to gender, food, and religion. But a final, extremely important topic remains: human happiness. This lecture takes a look at what the 4-field lens of anthropology—linguistics, biological anthropology, archaeology, and cultural anthropology—can teach us about happiness.

Linguistics

Linguistics can help us get a handle on the term *happiness*. If we go back and trace the origins of that word in every Indo-European language, we find a single answer. Even back to ancient Greek, the word for *happiness* is a cognate with the word for *luck*!

In Old English and Old Norse, the root *hap* means "luck" or "chance." The same goes in French and German.

As the centuries wore on, with the growth of the Abrahamic faiths in many places, happiness emerged as a religious sentiment describing the bliss of communion with God, either here on earth and/or in the afterlife.

But with the Enlightenment, we turned to the individual. Something happened that makes us think of happiness as something we cultivate. Now, when we're unhappy, we try to do things to get happy.

Many people in the world see happiness as being somewhere along this historical spectrum. There are plenty of cultures that are more in line with luck-based happiness versus contemporary Western constructions.

A cursory look into the linguistic evolution of the word *happiness* reveals that happiness is not simply a joyful feeling. It's the result of good living. Where Socrates would teach us that the path to happiness lies in the education of our desires, we can also see that happiness is about living.

Beyond our material and physical well-being on any given day, happiness comes from our relationships, our productivity, and our personal freedom. Happiness lines up with the Socratic view that we can make ourselves happy if we put in the effort (and, ironically, suffer quite a bit on the way).

The joy of raising a child, for example, is the ultimate source of happiness in many people's lives. But that happiness is built and grows over a lifetime, including painful bumps along the way.

Biological Anthropology

Biological anthropology enables us to examine happiness as a biological phenomenon. When we're happy and when we're laughing, our bodies produce brain molecules that are directly linked to euphoria or well-being. When people laugh, for example, they produce endorphins, which are natural opiates in terms of their chemical structure. They can help assuage physical and emotional pain.

People also produce dopamine, which is linked to pleasure seeking. In addition, they produce oxytocin, the so-called bonding and trust molecule. Other examples include substances like endocannabinoids, serotonin, and adrenaline.

In a 2012 study, scientists checked in on over 2000 participants from a wide variety of countries. They tracked down what made the participants feel happy. Specific activities produced higher happiness ratings. Making love was top on the list by quite a margin, but it wasn't the only "happy" activity. Listening to music, talking with a friend, and working out also appear to be happiness-producing activities.

Laughter can also help produce happiness. For example, the nonprofit organization Rx Laughter runs comedy therapy programs

Listening to music appears to be a happiness-producing activity.

for children with serious medical conditions. The organization also does collaborative research on happiness and healing with the UCLA Jonsson Comprehensive Cancer Center.

According to their research, patients in the Rx Laughter program experienced increased pain tolerance and reduced anxiety. They found that even kids who didn't audibly laugh out loud benefited from the program.

Archaeology

Archaeology focuses us on material culture, or artifacts. Using material remains, anthropologists can reconstruct the lives of people across the world and across the generations. In turn, anthropologists can watch for indicators that could be interpreted as happiness.

For example, Egyptologists might point to research on the popularity of senet, one of Ancient Egypt's favorite board games, as a window into the pursuit of happiness among the Ancient Egyptian masses.

Research has shown that our happiness is fed by our relationships. The archaeological record is unequivocal about why our happiness is so dependent upon the quality of close, face-to-face relationships.

Humans lived in small, hunter-gatherer bands for most of *Homo sapiens'* 200,000 years on earth. About 10,000 years ago, the rise of agriculture led to the eventual rise of urban centers, but most communities were rather small by today's standards.

That matters because *Homo sapiens* evolved as social animals. For thousands upon thousands of years, individual success was heavily dependent on communal cooperation. For our ancestors, the happiness experience would be rooted on the community side of the community-individual continuum.

Cultural Anthropology

It's tricky to identify and compare happiness across cultures. Unfortunately, cultural anthropologists haven't paid a lot of attention to happiness. But happiness research has taken place outside of anthropology.

As a whole, happiness research tends to focus on 2 main types of happiness: life satisfaction happiness and subjective happiness. Life satisfaction happiness is an assessment of a person's life in whole. Subjective happiness is more about the happy-to-sad spectrum and where a person feels they are on that scale from day to day.

Researchers use both of these categories to rank all the world's countries from the happiest to the most miserable.

One of the most comprehensive and data-driven ranking systems is the *World Happiness Report*, which has been publishing its findings since 2012. It measures both life satisfaction happiness and subjective happiness.

To navigate cultural and linguistic differences, the researchers boil subjective happiness down into a few revealing questions, like these:

- If you were in trouble, do you have relatives or friends you can count on to help you whenever you need them?
- Are you satisfied or dissatisfied with your freedom to choose what you do with your life?
- Have you donated to charity in the past month?

Life satisfaction happiness is more straightforward. The researchers simply ask people to rate their own happiness on a scale of 0 to 10, with 0 being the worst life imaginable and 10 being the best life imaginable.

For 2015, the mean happiness rating across all countries was 5.4. But massive differences are hidden in that statistic. For example, while North America weighs in at 7.1, sub-Saharan Africa is a meager 4.3.

Despite researchers' best efforts, identifying and measuring happiness is culturally complicated—and biased. These world rankings are based not only on people's responses to questions about their happiness, but also on life expectancy and GDP. Psychologists have proven that more money does not equate to more happiness, so it seems shortsighted to quantitatively discount the happiness of the majority world on the basis of GDP.

But even with unintentional cultural blinders and bias, the *World Happiness Report* is terrific. It produces more questions with each published edition, and the results have been fairly consistent over the years. And, just like anthropology, the more people critically test and correct their happiness theories and methods, the closer they'll get to a more inclusive approach.

In the 2016 report, a few interesting findings beg additional attention:

- There was a 4-point gap between top 10 and bottom 10 nations.

- Scandinavian countries dominate the top 5 happy slots, whereas Togo scored the lowest at 2.84.

- There was a net loss in happiness over the past decade for a handful of countries. These countries have been suffering greatly from enduring conflict or economic devastation: Yemen, Venezuela, Botswana, Saudi Arabia, Egypt, and Greece.

- After the Japan earthquake of 2011, generosity, trust, and solidarity during the crisis response led to increased happiness. This interesting

finding is certainly in line with the connection between happiness and community.

Happiness Examples: Bhutan and Okinawa

In the country of Bhutan, the people measure and actively work to increase what they call Gross National Happiness. The revered former king, Jigme Singye Wangchuck, abandoned the monarchy. But before he stepped out of his role, he helped lead the creation of a constitutional democracy.

The relatively new Bhutan government considers it the official responsibility of the government to create an environment for individuals to pursue happiness. They measure GDP too, but they place more value on the pursuit of happiness than the pursuit of sheer economic profit.

Another society with an interesting take on happiness can be found in Okinawa. This community, Ogimi-son, has the world's highest concentration of centenarians. These people live remarkably happy lives through a shared ethos of compassion through togetherness.

They take this ethos all the way to the grave. When people pass away in Ogimi-son, they are cremated, and their ashes are poured into a communal cemetery. Ogimi-son is a single community with a single destination that is clear from the start.

The Meaning

What does all this anthropology of happiness mean? Our reality is shaped by the language we use every day, and in particular the questions we ask. If our language is largely negative, it's no surprise that the world we see will seem negative too. Asking the wrong questions can mean we spend a lot of time and effort focusing our attention on all the wrong things.

Anthropology can be a great way to ask the "right" questions— the questions that reveal the unity and cultural diversity of humankind. They're the questions we've been answering all along in this course: Who are we? Where do we come from? How are we related to each other?

Perhaps the biggest human question is: What is the purpose of life? Everyone has to answer that for themselves, but the anthropology of happiness suggests that the more we search for an inclusive, universal expression of happiness, the more we'll see it as the fuel that sustains us.

Biologically, culturally, and emotionally, happiness keeps us healthy and motivates us to be more compassionate and connected to humankind. In a similar vein, the science of happiness shows us that there are definite connections between happiness, hope, gratitude, forgiveness, and altruism.

Suggested Reading

Collen, *10% Human*.

Hanh, *No Mud, No Lotus*.

Journal of Happiness Studies.

Ricard, *Happiness*.

Questions to Consider

1. How has humanity's definition of happiness changed since the years of our hunter-gatherer ancestors?

2. Is happiness a universal experience or does it differ from culture to culture?

3. How might anthropology help us increase happiness in our own lives?

Bibliography

Baker, Lee. *From Savage to Negro: Anthropology and the Construction of Race, 1896–1954*. Berkeley: University of California Press, 1998. Baker's essential study traces roles of early American anthropologists and the erroneous ideas that unscientifically divided our one human race, *Homo sapiens*, into multiple, socially constructed races.

Becker, Howard. *Art Worlds*. 25th anniversary ed. Berkeley: University of California Press, 2008. Sociologist Howard Becker's classic work helps visual anthropologists and others reconsider art not as objects produced by artists, but as collective action including artists, dealers, gallery managers, publishers, consumers, and just about anyone else engaged in the world of art.

Berwick, Robert and Noam Chomsky. *Why Only Us: Language and Evolution*. Cambridge, MA: MIT Press, 2015. Berwick, a computer scientist, and Chomsky, a celebrated linguist, join forces to explore humanity's unique biological foundations that render complex language possible.

Black, Edwin. *War Against the Weak: Eugenics and America's Campaign to Create a Master Race*. Westport, CT: Dialog Press, 2012. Edwin Black recounts the seldom-told story of the early days of genetics research and the direct connections between the American eugenics movement and the atrocities of Nazi Germany's concentration camps and holocaust.

Bolotin, Norman and Christine Laing. *The World's Columbian Exposition: The Chicago World's Fair of 1893*. Champaign: University of Illinois Press, 2002. Take a beautifully illustrated trip with Bolotin and Laing to the 1893 Chicago World's Fair where early anthropologists first introduced the American public to what was an emerging academic discipline.

Bostrom, Nick and Milan M. Cirkovic. *Global Catastrophic Risks*. Oxford: Oxford University Press, 2011. To assess the sobering existential threats facing humankind in the 21st century, Bostrom and Cirkovic turn to 25 leading experts to suss out the potential end of our species via nuclear war, biological weapons, terrorism, asteroids, social collapse, the rise of artificial intelligence, and more.

Brown, Peter J. and Svea Closser. *Understanding and Applying Medical Anthropology*. 3rd ed. New York: Routledge, 2016. Used in classrooms across the United States and world, this classic medical anthropology reader is one of the best and most efficient ways to survey the remarkable breadth and contributions of one of the most popular specializations in contemporary anthropology.

Burling, Robbins. *The Talking Ape: How Language Evolved.* Oxford: Oxford University Press, 2007. Thinking back on the origins of language, Burling shares some fascinating theories on how and why humans first started using words and grammar.

Clarke, Kamari Maxine. *Fictions of Justice: The International Criminal Court and the Challenge of Legal Pluralism in Sub-Saharan Africa*. Cambridge, U.K.: Cambridge University Press, 2009. A riveting example of legal anthropology at work in the 21st century, this compelling study of the International Criminal Court demonstrates that ideas like human rights and justice are culture bound, and thus, far more complicated (and political) than one might think.

Cleveland, David. *Balancing on a Planet: The Future of Food and Agriculture*. Berkeley: University of California Press, 2013. In this integrative, forward-thinking study, David Cleveland looks to the future of food production by embracing lessons and practices from scientific and small-scale farming systems.

Cohen, Mark Nathan and George Armelagos. *Paleopathology at the Origins of Agriculture*. Cambridge, MA: Academic Press, 1984. Considered a foundational text in bioarchaeology, this volume brings together authors from across the discipline to uncover fascinating discoveries about the impact of agriculture on the health of early farmers in Asia, the Middle East, Europe, and the Americas.

Collen, Alanna. *10% Human: How Your Body's Microbes Hold the Key to Health and Happiness*. Repr. ed. New York: Harper, 2016. From a biological perspective, biologist Alanna Collen explains that, remarkably, our happiness (and much more) has roots in the microbes our bodies carry.

Crawford, David. *Moroccan Households in the World Economy: Labor and Inequality in a Berber Village*. Baton Rouge: Louisiana State University, 2008. This thoughtfully crafted Moroccan ethnography provides an excellent example of how Steward's cultural ecology continues to influence 21st-century anthropology.

Darwin, Charles. *The Origin of Species*. 150th anniversary ed. New York: Signet, 2003. One of the foundational texts of modern biology and anthropology, Darwin's most celebrated title ushered in a new era in science, an era engrossed with deciphering the mysteries of biological evolution.

Dawkins, Richard and Yan Wong. *The Ancestor's Tale: A Pilgrimage to the Dawn of Evolution*. Rev. ed. New York: Mariner, 2016. Inspired by the form of Chaucer's *Canterbury Tales*, the authors of this meticulous account retell the story of life on Earth.

De Waal, Frans. *The Bonobo and the Atheist: In Search of Humanism Among the Primates*. New York: Norton, 2014. Known for his creative and insightful writing on primates, Frans de Waal unveils the biological and cultural roots of human morality in the observed behavior of the primate order and the wider animal kingdom.

Errington, Shelly. *The Death of Authentic Primitive Art and Other Tales of Progress*. Berkeley: University of California Press, 1998. Errington examines the category of primitive art to reveal it as a flawed and inadequate classification that tells more about the worldview of 20th-century anthropologists rather than the cultures and artists who produce what we once called primitive art.

Evans-Pritchard, Edward. *The Nuer: A Description of the Livelihood and Political Institutions of a Nilotic People*. New York: Oxford University Press, 1969 (orig. 1940). A revered model of early-20th-century ethnography, Evans-Pritchard's detailed account of the Nuer people of East Africa examines their religious practices, social structure, and much more.

Fagan, Brian. *Ancient Lives: An Introduction to Archaeology and Prehistory*. 4th ed. Upper Saddle River, NJ: Prentice Hall, 2009. World-renowned archaeologist Brian Fagan lays out the basic ideas and methods of archaeology as he surveys some of the biggest developments in human prehistory, including the spread of modern humanity and the emergence of agriculture.

Ferllini, Roxana. *Silent Witness: How Forensic Anthropology is Used to Solve the World's Toughest Crimes*. 2nd ed. Ontario: Firefly Books, 2012. This well-illustrated volume describes specific techniques and procedures used by forensic anthropologists through a discussion of 32 remarkable cases ranging from a train collision and airplane crash to genocide and serial killers.

Fouts, Roger and Stephen Tukel Mills. *Next of Kin: My Conversations with Chimpanzees*. New York: William Morrow, 1998. One of the first primatologists to work with apes using sign language, Roger Fouts, along with his coauthor, share terrific stories of friendship, humor, and discovery through interspecies communication and ape conservation.

Frazer, James. *The Golden Bough*. Abridged ed. Mineola, NY: Dover Press, 2002 (originally written in 1890). This early anthropological classic captured the imagination of many of the scholars who went on to establish anthropology as an academic discipline, and Frazer's compendium of the various beliefs and social institutions of world cultures was so popular and comprehensive that it eventually grew into a 12-volume epic.

Goodall, Jane. *In the Shadow of Man.* New York: Mariner, 2010. Starting with the story of a life-altering conversation with and suggestion from Dr. Louis Leakey, Goodall tells the inspirational story of how her life among the chimpanzees of Gombe unfolded, and how she came to know these chimps as complicated individuals and even toolmakers.

Graeber, David. *Debt: The First 5,000 Years*. New York: Melville House, 2014. Graeber's comprehensive history of debt draws on hard evidence from archaeology, cultural anthropology, and more to challenge and revise one of the foundational theories in classical economics, namely that human exchange started with bartering prior to the creation of debt and currency.

Graf, Kelly, Caroline Ketron, and Michael Waters, eds. *Paleoamerican Odyssey*. College Station: Texas A&M Press, 2014. By analyzing ancient skeletal remains as well as the genomes of living populations, the authors provide remarkable new insight on the peopling of the Americas.

Hanh, Thich Naht. *No Mud, No Lotus: The Art of Transforming Suffering*. Berkeley: Parallax Press, 2014. This world-renowned monk and former associate of Martin Luther King, Jr. explains an ironic secret to the art of happiness: acknowledging and then transforming our suffering.

Harari, Yuvai Noah. *Sapiens: A Brief History of Humankind.* New York: Harper, 2015. Harari boils down over a century of discoveries and evidence on the origins and spread of *Homo sapiens* in a compelling narrative that underscores the remarkable journey that created our modern humanity.

Harris, Marvin. *Good to Eat: Riddles of Food and Culture*. Long Grove, IL: Waveland, 1998. This engaging example of Harris's cultural materialism decodes food taboos and preferences from throughout the world, from the sacred cow in India to the troubles many parents have getting their children to eat spinach.

Hart, Keith. *The Memory Bank: Money in an Unequal World*. Cambridge, UK: Profile Books, 1999. Hart examined the impact of revolutionary technologies like the Internet, predicting that these changes will usher in truer forms of economic democracy across the globe.

Harvey, Joy Dorothy. *Almost a Man of Genius: Clémence Royer, Feminism, and Nineteenth-Century Science*. New Brunswick: Rutgers University Press, 1997. A little-known feminist and scientist hero, Clémence Royer once served as Darwin's French translator, but her contributions and critiques of the male-dominated scientific community were revolutionary and, arguably, over a century ahead of the mainstream.

Henley, Paul. *The Adventure of the Real: Jean Rouch and the Craft of Ethnographic Cinema*. Chicago: University of Chicago Press, 2010. This is an essential account of one of the most remarkable ethnographic filmmakers of the 20th century, whose methods and work did nothing short of launching the genre we know today as cinema verite.

Henrich, Joseph. *The Secret of Our Success: How Culture Is Driving Human Evolution, Domesticating Our Species, and Making Us Smarter*. New Brunswick, NJ: Princeton University Press, 2015. Our evolution as social beings produced a collective intelligence that, like cultural DNA, has fueled our success as a species that builds on the technological achievements of past generations.

Hrdy, Sarah Blaffer. *Mothers and Others: The Evolutionary Origins of Mutual Understanding*. Washington DC: Harvard University Press, 2009. Hrdy looks to primates and human history to reconstruct the development of our capacity to care for each other, and to examine our modern emotional state as human beings.

Humphrey, Caroline and Stephen Hugh-Jones. *Barter, Exchange and Value: An Anthropological Approach*. Cambridge, UK: Cambridge University Press, 1992. Humphrey and Hugh-Jones provide one of the most thorough and evidence-based discussions of the anthropology and history of barter, and they demonstrate that this human institution is far more complex than one may think.

Hurston, Zora Neale. *Mules and Men*. New York: Harper Perennial, 2008. Hurston returned to her hometown in southern Florida to document the rich oral traditions, wisdom, humor, and resilience of Black communities in the Deep South.

Jablonski, Nina. *Living Color: The Biological and Social Meaning of Skin Color*. Berkeley: University of California Press, 2012. Jablonski provides a definitive evolutionary account of the development of diverse skin colors across the human family, and she shows us how this basic adaptation to sunlight has impacted our sociocultural relations and health in profound ways that contradict popular constructions of race.

Jennings, Justin. *Killing Civilization: A Reassessment of Early Urbanism and Its Consequences*. Albuquerque: University of New Mexico Press, 2016. Jennings reviews excavation and survey data from Cahokia (Mississippi Valley), Jenne-jeno (Mali), Tiwanaku/Tiahuanaco (South America), and elsewhere to develop new perspectives on the nature and consequences of these celebrated early civilizations.

Journal of Happiness Studies: An Interdisciplinary Forum on Subjective Well-Being. Dordrecht, Netherlands: Springer, 2000 to present. This peer review journal features scientific research into understanding the happiness spectrum.

King, Barbara. *Evolving God: A Provocative View on the Origins of Religion*. New York: Doubleday, 2007. Noted primatologist Barbara King's remarkable study incorporates non-human ape behavior, archaeology, and even biology to give us a comprehensive and integrative window into the origins of the human religious experience.

Kolbert, Elizabeth. *The Sixth Extinction: An Unnatural History*. Repr. ed. London: Picador, 2015. Kolbert's widely popular and rather disquieting assessment of the impact of humankind on Earth warns us with urgency that previous mass extinctions foreshadow yet another massive die-off that, quite likely, could include *Home sapiens*.

Kroeber, Alfred and Clyde Kluckholn. *Culture: A Critical Review of Concepts and Definitions*. New Haven, CT: The Peabody Museum, 1952. In the twilight of his career, early anthropologist Alfred Kroeber worked with Cylde Kluckholn to document the evolution of anthropology through an investigation of the ever increasing ways that anthropologists conceive and define culture.

Kurzweil, Ray. *The Singularity Is Near: When Humans Transcend Biology*. London: Penguin Books, 2006. Technologist and futurist Ray Kurzweil offers his optimism that humankind could achieve an immortality of sorts through the exponential growth and application of genetics, nanotechnology, and robotics.

Lacy, Scott. "Nanotechnology and Food Security: What Scientists Can Learn from Malian Farmers" in *Can Emerging Technologies Make a Difference in Development?* Eds. E. Parker and R. Appelbaum, 86–98. New York: Routledge. In narrative form, this chapter recounts the author's work as a bridge builder, connecting knowledge experts across linguistic, cultural, and geographic barriers.

Leick, Gwendolyn. *Mesopotamia: The Invention of the City*. London: Penguin, 2003. Archaeologist Gwendolyn Leick takes us to Mesopotamia and the first urban revolution to help us understand what life was like in 10 ancient Mesopotamian villages.

Lévi-Strauss, Claude. *The Elementary Structures of Kinship*. Boston: Beacon, 1969 (orig. 1949). Reviewing an impressive array of ethnographic evidence and accounts, Levi-Strauss interprets a classic anthropological theme, kinship, as a form of exchange that reveals what he described as a universal basis for marriage prohibition (e.g. incest avoidance) and a formalization of male-female relationships.

Little, Walter and Timothy Smith. *Mayas in Postwar Guatemala: Harvest of Violence Revisited*. Tuscaloosa: University of Alabama Press, 2009. Little and Smith uncover the non-violent resilience of Mayan people and communities to improve political, social, and economic conditions in postwar Guatemala, despite the enduring violence and insecurity they grapple with daily.

Lowie, Robert H. *Primitive Religion*. New York: New York: Liveright Publishing Corporation, 1948 (originally published in 1924). This early classic on the anthropology of religion takes the reader on an epic journey across the world to learn about the diverse religious beliefs and practices of humankind.

Malinowski, Bronisław. *Argonauts of the Western Pacific*. Long Grove, IL: Waveland, 1984 (originally published in 1922). Considered the go-to guide for foundational principles in anthropology field research, Malinowski's pioneering and comprehensive study of the Trobriand Islanders cemented participant observation as the hallmark of cultural anthropology.

Manhein, Mary. *The Bone Lady: Life as a Forensic Anthropologist*. Baton Rouge: Louisiana State University Press, 1999. As someone who has worked on hundreds and hundreds of cases, forensic anthropology superstar Mary Manhein artfully tells the story of some of the most remarkable moments of her career—including the recovery and identification of the 7 astronauts who perished in the 2003 *Columbia* disaster.

Marion, Jonathan and Jerome Crowder. *Visual Research: A Concise Introduction to Thinking Visually*. London: Bloomsbury Academic, 2013. This comprehensive guidebook for visual anthropologists examines the potential opportunities and pitfalls of doing visual anthropology research in an age of globally ubiquitous cellphones and other image-making technologies.

Mintz, Sidney. *Sweetness and Power: The Place of Sugar in Modern History*. London: Penguin, 1986. This celebrated study by Mintz digs deep into the history of sugar and reveals that a comprehensive examination of a single, global commodity can reveal a compelling history of the exploitative nature of international relations and exploitation.

Nelson, Sarah Milledge. *Women in Antiquity: Theoretical Approaches to Gender and Archaeology*. Lanham, Maryland: AltaMira Press,

2007. Through archaeology we can see that contemporary ideas and constructions of gender and womenhood are anything but consistent.

Netting, Robert. *Smallholders, Householders: Farm Families and the Ecology of Intensive, Sustainable Agriculture*. Redwood City: Stanford University Press, 1993. Integrating case studies from across the globe, Netting's classic text makes a compelling and thorough case for the efficiency and sustainability of small-scale farmer over industrial agriculture.

Newkirk, Pamela. *Spectacle: The Astonishing Life of Ota Benga*. New York: Amistad, 2015. A surprisingly revealing and tragic account of the early days of modern science and regrettably unscientific constructions of race.

Nolan, Riall. *Development Anthropology*. Boulder, CO: Westview Press, 2001. Applied anthropologist Riall Nolan describes how international development projects work, including the roles and contributions of anthropologists.

Nordstrom, Carolyn. *A Different Kind of War Story*. Philadelphia: University of Pennsylvania Press, 1997. In this riveting ethnography of civil war in Mozambique, Nordstrom shows us how, in the face of extreme violence and danger, regular citizens emerge as remarkable heroes, healers, and peacemakers.

Packard, Randall M. *The Making of a Tropical Disease: A Short History of Malaria*. Baltimore: Johns Hopkins University Press, 2011. In this essential resource for anyone curious about medical anthropology, Packard explains the social and natural complexities that foster the spread of malaria, which still kills 1 to 3 million people a year.

Pauketat, Timothy. *Cahokia: Ancient America's Great City on the Mississippi*. Repr. ed. London: Penguin Books, 2010. Archaeologist Timothy Pauketat goes back 1000 years ago to unearth a great Mississippi Valley civilization with extensive trade relations, remarkable technological innovation, and a massive earthen pyramid.

Peletz, Michael. *Gender Pluralism: Southeast Asia Since Early Modern Times*. London: Routledge, 2009. In this historical and ethnographic study of gender pluralism in Southeast Asia, Peletz examines the inconsistent ways people construct human diversity in ways that lead us to reject some forms of human variation while embracing others.

Peterson, Dale and Richard Wrangham. *Demonic Males: Apes and the Origins of Human Violence*. New York: Mariner, 1997. Peterson and Wrangham turn to non-human apes to explore the potential biological and evolutionary roots of human violence.

Podolefsky, Aaron, Peter J. Brown, and Scott M. Lacy. *Applying Anthropology*. New York: McGraw-Hill, 2012. This popular reader contains compelling chapters written by a host of anthropologists who take you right into the field to see the myriad ways different anthropologists apply the 4 fields of their discipline to demonstrate anthropology's unique roles as a tool for social transformation and human understanding.

Price, David. *Weaponizing Anthropology: Social Science in Service of the Militarized State*. Petrolia, CA: CounterPunch Books, 2011. In this revealing and comprehensive history of the complex and often nefarious relationship between anthropologists and the CIA, FBI, and US military, David Price critically examines the ethical and practical dimensions of putting anthropology to use in war zones and counterinsurgency programs.

Redfield, Robert. *The Little Community and Peasant Society and Culture*. Repr. ed. Chicago: University of Chicago Press, 1989. This reprint edition includes 2 of Redfield's foundational and remarkably influential case studies on the nature of what he referred to as peasant communities.

Ricard, Mathieu. *Happiness: A Guide to Developing Life's Most Important Skill*. Boston: Little, Brown and Company, 2007. Drawing on his experience as both a molecular biologist and a Buddhist monk, Ricard (who has been described by scientists as the happiest man alive) reveals what it takes to achieve a lasting happiness.

Richards, Audrey. *Land, Labour, and Diet in Northern Rhodesia: An Economic Study of the Bemba Tribe*. London: Oxford University Press, 1939. Based on extensive participant observation fieldwork among agriculturalists in East Africa, Richards set a new anthropological standard by incorporating diet and other factors into her carefully documented study of the social and economic life of the Bemba.

Rodney, Walter. *How Europe Underdeveloped Africa*. Washington DC: Howard University Press, 1982. Used by social scientists and scholars of development studies, Rodney's classic text provides a view of international development from the perspective of the so-called third world.

Roughgarden, Joan. *Evolution's Rainbow: Diversity, Gender, and Sexuality in Nature and People*. 10th anniversary edition. Berkeley: University of California Press, 2013. Compiling a remarkable array of scientific studies on humans and the animal kingdom at large, Roughgarden's seminal and unparalleled study helps us better articulate the diversity of humankind with an exhaustive deconstruction and re-articulation of biological sex, sexuality, and gender.

Russell, Bernard. *Research Methods in Anthropology*. 4th ed. Lanham, Maryland: AltaMira, 2006. This definitive go-to guide for all anthropologists is a rich treasure trove that outlines the anthropological method.

Shanahan, Murray. *The Technological Singularity*. Cambridge, MA: MIT Press, 2015. Shannahan peers into the potential future of humankind, not to sensationally stir up fear, but to soberly consider a number of scenarios that could result from the exponential growth in artificial intelligence.

Shostak. Marjorie. *Nisa: The Life and Words of a !Kung Woman*. Cambridge, MA: Harvard University Press, 1981. Shostak lived amongst hunter-gatherers in the Kalahari and gained unparalleled insight into foraging lifestyles by documenting the surprisingly candid life history of a female hunter-gatherer named Nisa.

Steadman, Dawnie Wolf. *Hard Evidence: Case Studies in Forensic Anthropology*. 2nd ed. New York: Routledge, 2008. By exploring numerous cases, this collection of readings exposes the reader to the dynamics of forensics anthropology, casting some light on what it's like to work in this fascinating field.

Sterling, Eleanor, Nora Bynum, and Mary Blair. *Primate Ecology and Conservation: A Handbook of Techniques*. Oxford: Oxford University Press, 2013. From planning field research to observation, data collection, and lab analysis, this reference book surveys the amazing methodological range of primatologists concerned with primate ecology and conservation.

Steward, Julian. *Theory of Culture Change: The Methodology of Multilinear Evolution*. Repr. ed. Champaign: University of Illinois Press, 1990. Spanning 2 decades of work, this collection articulates how Steward unpacks and understands the intricacies of culture change.

Stocking, George. *Observers Observed: Essays on Ethnographic Fieldwork*. Madison: University of Wisconsin Press, 1983. Stocking's edited collection of essays portrays the inner lives of a number of anthropologists, including Franz Boas, and in so doing reveals the challenges and triumphs of ethnographic fieldwork.

Stocking, George W., Jr. *Victorian Anthropology*. New York: The Free Press, 1987. Stocking documents the troubling origins of anthropology in the Victorian Era, when armchair scholars typically relied on the extremely biased accounts of intrepid travelers and missionaries to understand the cultures of far-away people.

Stringer, Chris. *Lone Survivors: How We Came to Be the Only Humans on Earth*. New York: St. Martin's Griffin, 2013. Based on a stunning reevaluation of the fossil record, archaeological sites, and recent DNA research, paleoanthropologist Chris Stringer revises long-held theories on how *Homo sapiens* exclusively came to populate nearly every corner of the globe.

Tannen, Deborah. *That's Not What I Meant!: How Conversational Style Makes or Breaks Relationships*. New York: William Morrow, 2011. Linguist Deborah Tannen has some important lessons to help you maintain healthy relationships through communication, including ways to make sure the things you say to your loved ones are actually what they hear.

Tattersall, Ian. *Masters of the Planet: The Search for Our Human Origins.* New York: St. Martin's Griffin, 2013. Tattersal, curator emeritus of the American Museum of Natural History, peers into the extensive fossil record of humanity to reveal the truly remarkable and rapid rise of *Homo sapiens*.

Tylor, Edward B. *Primitive Culture*. Vols. 1 and 2. New York: Harper & Brothers, 1958 (originally published in 1873). In one of the original anthropological texts, Tylor spells out his enduring definition of culture, and tirelessly reviews a wide variety of sources on what he characterized as primitive cultures throughout the world.

Waters, Michael and Thomas Jennings. *The Hogeye Clovis Cache.* College Station: Texas A&M University Press, 2015. Waters and Jennings help us understand one of the original American techno-cultural trends, the Clovis point.

Wilkinson, Iain and Arthur Kleinmann. *A Passion for Society: How We Think about Human Suffering*. Berkeley: University of California Press, 2016. With a medical anthropology giant as one of its co-authors, this text makes the case for emboldening contemporary social science by returning to its roots as a discipline that is fundamentally committed to caring for others and critically fostering a more human world.

Image Credits

Page 165: © digitalskillet/iStock/Thinkstock.

Page 168: © emarto/iStock/Thinkstock.

Page 170: © foto_abstract/iStock/Thinkstock.

Page 175: © Amit Somvanshi/Thinkstock.

Page 177: © debstheleo/iStock/Thinkstock.

Page 179: © Media Bank/Photos.com/Thinkstock.

Page 181: © sihasakprachum/iStock/Thinkstock.

Page 182: © AlexRaths/iStock/Thinkstock.

Page 186: © Jupiterimages/Creatas/Thinkstock.

Page 188: © Jack Hollingsworth/DigitalVision/Thinkstock.

Page 191: © william87/iStock/Thinkstock.

Page 193: © Rawpixel Ltd/iStock/Thinkstock.

NOTES

NOTES

NOTES

NOTES